THE IMPACT OF CULTURE ON
ORGANIZATIONAL DECISION MAKING

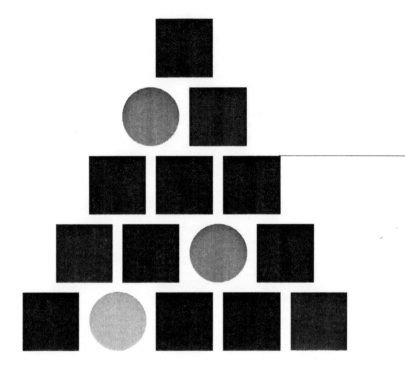

THE IMPACT OF CULTURE ON ORGANIZATIONAL DECISION MAKING

Theory and Practice in Higher Education

William G. Tierney

STERLING, VIRGINIA

Sty/us

COPYRIGHT © 2008 BY WILLIAM G. TIERNEY

Published by Stylus Publishing, LLC
22883 Quicksilver Drive
Sterling, Virginia 20166-2102

Library of Congress Cataloging-in-Publication-Data
Tierney, William G.
   The impact of culture on organizational decision making: theory and practice in higher education / William G. Tierney.—1st ed.
     p. cm.
   Includes bibliographical references and index.
   ISBN 978–1-57922-287-1 (pbk. : alk. paper)
   1. Universities and colleges—Administration—Decision making—Social aspects.
2. College environment.   I. Title.
LB2341.T586   2008
378.1'01—dc22   2007048784

13-digit ISBN: 978-1-57922-287-1 (paper)

Printed in the United States of America

All first editions printed on acid free paper
that meets the American National Standards Institute
Z39-48 Standard.

First Edition, 2008

10 9 8 7 6 5 4 3 2 1

CONTENTS

THE STRANGE CASE OF
ORGANIZATIONAL CULTURE

His mind . . . was busy in endeavoring to frame
some scheme into which all these strange and
apparently disconnected episodes could be
fitted.

—Doctor Watson, about Sherlock Holmes
(Doyle, 1902, p. 72)

Those who work in, study, and lead colleges and universities undoubtedly identify with the comment Doctor Watson has made
about his friend, Sherlock Holmes. A donor berates the president
because the football team lost a game and threatens to cancel his gift for a
new student center. A speaker comes to campus who denounces the United
States and the mayor of the city then denounces the faculty for inviting the
speaker; the faculty, in turn, denounces the university president for not supporting academic freedom. The campus library committee dissolves in a dispute between those who want to continue buying paper books and those
who want to go digital. A professor shoots a gun out the window as a demon-
stration of fear and paranoia in her intro to psychology classroom, the campus police arrest her, and the Faculty Senate calls for the resignation of the
head of campus security because he has chilled the climate for free speech on
campus. A student has a bicycle accident and may be paralyzed for life, and
the campus has a candlelight vigil for him where 1,000 people show up. A
professor announces her retirement after four decades of teaching in the
Writing Program, and her former students return to campus for a celebratory
party; one of the participants has just won the Pulitzer Prize.

All of these "strange and apparently disconnected episodes" could happen on any number of campuses. The challenge for those of us who study

or work on such a campus is to try to figure out not only what holds the campus together, but how to strengthen the social glue so that the fabric of the institution is stronger tomorrow than it was yesterday. Such a challenge has less to do with facts and figures, bottom lines, or chains of command, and more to do with what I think of as an organization's culture. The idea of an organization's culture is not unlike the culture of a particular group.

When I graduated from college and joined the Peace Corps I ended up in the Atlas Mountains of Morocco. I was the only foreigner who lived in Tahala, a small Berber village nestled in the foothills and a day's drive to anything resembling a city. Anyone who has traveled abroad, especially to countries and cultures particularly different from one's own, undoubtedly has faced the sort of disorientation I encountered as a 21-year-old living abroad for the first time in my life. Social roles were different. The way people interacted with one another varied from what I expected. My sense of right and wrong, good and bad, were often in conflict with how my new neighbors acted. How I communicated with everyone was different; frequently I said or did something that I thought was completely innocuous or innocent only to discover that I had made yet another faux pas.

Culture is best understood when we transgress boundaries because, at those moments, individuals are clear that their cultural sensibility is in conflict with the accepted norms. However, culture is more than simply a list of dos and don'ts about how to act when abroad as if all that is needed is a Miss Manners book on cross-cultural etiquette. Instead, culture is more useful to think of as an interpretation that takes place on a daily basis among the members of a particular group. True, ceremonies, rituals, and traditions pervade a culture, but how members of a group make sense of and interpret those events also in part depends on the individuals currently involved and the current contexts in which they occur. From this perspective culture is neither static nor monolithic. Men and women, for example, may interpret the same event in an entirely different manner. Fifty years ago, men or women may have interpreted the same event differently from their counterparts today. Culture is in constant flux and reinterpretation.

An understanding of an organization's culture enables individuals to think of the organization more as an interpretive undertaking than a rationalized structure with clear decision-making processes. Anyone who moves from one institution to another knows that differences exist and that the new campus takes some getting used to—whether it be the manner in which the faculty interact with one another; the type of students at the institution; the relationships between the administration and faculty; or any number of microscopic topics, such as what events individuals are supposed to attend or even whether one eats lunch with others or at one's desk. The ability to think of the organization as a culture also helps individuals consider how seemingly disconnected episodes might actually fit together.

The study of organizational culture was a relatively new topic when I entered the academy in the 1980s. Culture was thought to be the domain of anthropologists who studied "exotic" tribes; at the time, rational decision making was the province of modern organizations and those who studied them. Strategic planning was all the rage, but the manner in which it was done involved an institution's leaders clarifying lines of authority and deciding which choices to make. In effect, a handful of an institution's leaders decided the course the institution was to take and everyone else followed. Usually, the institution followed a path that had been set; the status quo was the norm.

Since that time the study of culture has advanced a great deal, and individuals increasingly have moved away from linear and formalized decision-making structures and toward flatter, more collaborative undertakings. An understanding of culture has become essential for those who seek to understand how to foment change in the organization. Higher education is undergoing as significant a period of turbulence and innovation as at any time in the last 50 years. The status quo is no longer tenable, and of consequence, individuals have tried to figure out what might enable the campus to move forward rather than remain wedded to the norm. The point is not so much to drop everything that the institution once did, but to communicate to insiders and outsiders what the organization values and how it is different from other institutions. The result is a renewed interest in organizational culture.

This book discusses the various facets of organizational culture in three parts. The first part of the book opens with a discussion of how I define the culture of a postsecondary institution. In "Facts and Constructs" I point out how different an interpretive perspective is from a realist perspective. Proponents of realism believe organizational reality exists, whereas interpretivists do not. The chapter points out that a cultural perspective affects not only how researchers study the problems in an organization but also how the organization's actors act in it. Chapter 3, "Organizational Culture in Higher

Education," offers the reader a way to think about culture in academic organizations. Just as an anthropologist has particular terms he or she uses when studying a traditional culture, I suggest what terms are essential to consider when analyzing a college or university. An anthropologist who conducts an ethnography in a village, for example, undoubtedly will write about some aspects of kinships and ritual. To avoid such a discussion would be an oversight. Similarly, if we study a postsecondary institution and avoid the topic of the institution's mission, we would be remiss. The point, of course, is not to say that one or another mission is "good" or "bad," but, instead, to come to terms with how the "villagers"—those in the organization—use the term. I call upon data from a yearlong study to highlight the components of culture.

In Part Two we move from definitional terms to specific issues and problems. Chapter 4, "Academic Work and Institutional Culture," investigates how the institution's actors make sense of the curriculum in relation to the overarching mission of the organization. The challenge in the text is to come to terms with the manner in which an organization's participants define knowledge. I challenge the idea that the disciplines—those knowledge-producing units that were beyond the confines of an organization—develop knowledge. I also quarrel with the assumption that a postsecondary institution is merely where knowledge gets transferred to the consumer by way of curricula. Instead, I suggest that a college or university plays a role in defining knowledge based on its own culture and mores. A curriculum is an ideological statement that derives from the organizational participants' understanding of the curricula. The point is less that each institution is different, or "to each his own," and rather that knowledge is constantly redefined. One place where these definitions get worked out is at the curricular level in a postsecondary institution.

In chapters 5, 6, and 7, I discuss various aspects of student and faculty life. In "An Anthropological Analysis of Student Participation in College," I critique college-going models that use cultural terms (such as rites of passage) but fail to view such terms from a cultural perspective. I call upon data from my work with Native American youth to point out how different conceptual models of individuals based on their own unique cultures frequently come into conflict when they arrive on a mainstream campus. The challenge, I suggest, is that cultural models of assimilation create problems for those who are different—frequently students of color. The need for them is to undergo a cultural suicide of sorts, where they need to conform to dominant norms that may be in conflict with their own internalized sense of how to act.

Such an observation sheds light on the idea of organizational socialization. Rather than simply assume that new recruits need to be assimilated to the organization, I consider ways for an organization's participants to think of culture as multivocal, a place where creativity and differences may flourish. Colleges and universities are best when they are able to organize around the idea of difference, rather than conformity, but such a point seems at odds with the notion of culture where bonds of socialization tie people together. Indeed, the culture of the army may be easier to understand insofar as the norms are clearly articulated and the idea of socialization in large part pertains to figuring out how to get recruits inducted into the ideology of the group. However, in knowledge-creating organizations such as colleges or universities, the challenge is not assimilation but creativity. Creativity and innovation are particularly important in organizations not wedded to the status quo. In the 21st century, postsecondary institutions need to change if they are to succeed. The result is that we need a culture geared toward innovation rather than stasis. In large part, the second part of the book considers what such a culture looks like and how socialization functions to enable what I call "cultural integrity," where an individual maintains his or her own sense of self but also comes to terms with the culture of the organization.

One key component of culture that advances or retards organizational learning is communication, and in chapter 8, I offer an analysis of communication based on work I conducted with my colleague, James T. Minor, about governance and decision making. Communication, we argue, is not simply the pronouncements a college president makes at highly ceremonial occasions such as graduations, but also how individuals interact with one another on a daily basis. Communication occurs on multiple levels and in multiple forms. To understand the culture of an organization, an analyst needs to come to terms with how the organization's participants communicate with one another. At a time when e-mail has become ubiquitous and people are as likely to have a teleconference as a face-to-face meeting, communication is changing in both speed and delivery modes. The challenge in the chapter has less to do with stating that one form is better than another and more to do with suggesting that communication is essential for good governance; if we are not more focused on how communication is tied to the organization's culture, we run the risk of ineffectiveness. Good communication is not a cure-all, we argue, but bad communication is sure to make innovation that much more difficult.

I continue this line of thought in the final chapter. One of the unique characteristics of a college or university is the decision-making apparatus used to reach decisions about big and little issues. The idea of shared governance is both emblematic of organizational culture and "real" in the sense that it suggests the structures individuals employ to reach decisions. At times critics have suggested that shared governance is outmoded and too lethargic in a world where faster decision making needs to take place. Others have observed that the business world is becoming more like academe; businesses are more participative and less hierarchical. Both observations, while correct, miss the point. Shared governance is a cultural artifact of the organization. I do not wish to embalm the idea as something sacred and untouchable, but we are also mistaken when we look on it as nothing more than a decision-making structure. "The way we do things around here" goes to the heart of an organization's culture. The challenge is to consider cultural artifacts in the changing times in which they exist and to think about how to improve them, rather than simply acting in an instrumental manner as if all we are doing is changing the stoplights on a street corner to make them more efficient.

In sum, organizational culture is that "scheme" for the latter-day Sherlock Holmes who studies or works in academic institutions. When we utilize a cultural perspective, we have a better understanding of how seemingly unconnected acts and events fall into place and, more important, how to help the organization's participants move forward. If the status quo is untenable in a fast-changing environment such as that in which we now find ourselves, then we need an institution's members to be able to not rely on tired assumptions about "that's the way we've always done it." Culture is dynamic and ever changing. In this book I surely do not offer a cookbook of recipes to follow, but the chapters afford us the ability to think about the various aspects of culture that enable individuals to come together and then move forward.

Reference

Doyle, A. C. (1902). *The hound of the Baskervilles: Another adventure of Sherlock Holmes.* New York: Signet Classics.

PART ONE

DEFINING ORGANIZATIONAL CULTURE

2

FACTS AND CONSTRUCTS
Defining Reality in Higher Education Organizations

O ne subject of current debate among organizational theorists is whether environments are objective or socially constructed phenomena. In this chapter, I consider the implications for researchers and administrators if we interpret the organizational environment of higher education as socially constructed or "enacted" (Smircich & Stubbart, 1985). Although this interpretive perspective has been mentioned in some higher education literature (Cameron, 1984; Chaffee, 1985; Chaffee & Tierney, 1988; Tierney, 1988a; Whetten & Cameron, 1985), the implications for higher education researchers and administrators have not been adequately explored. The supposition that environments are socially constructed implies an alternative orientation to problem solving and raises new research questions.

I first differentiate between objective and enacted environments. Arguing that organizations are socially constructed, I then consider the implications of an interpretive perspective for researchers. Finally, I consider managing an organization in an enacted environment and suggest that the effect of differing perceptions of environments on college and university organizations has important consequences for the higher education community.

Organizational Perceptions of the Environment
The Objective Environment

Although many interpretations of an objective environment are possible, I will apply an ecological/evolutionary framework to the analysis of higher

Note: This chapter originally appeared as Tierney, W. G. (1987). Facts and constructs: Defining reality in higher education organizations. *The Review of Higher Education, 11*(1), 61–73.

education environments. From the vantage point of an objectivist, organizational participants regard the environment as a complex, ever-changing set of consumer preferences. Constituencies demand organizational action to bring the institution into equilibrium with its environment. In other words, the organization adapts to the demands of the environment. One might think of such a view in biological terms. Higher education consists of different "species" (e.g., liberal arts, vocational) that undergo transformation due to the constantly changing environment.

An understanding of the environment as ecological is predicated on the assumption that an organization is a rational, objective, "real" entity. The environment is dynamic and ever changing. Rather than assume that the organization must *deal* with the external, the assumption is that the organization must *change* with it (Chaffee, 1985). The structure of the environment is composed of a finite number of elements that already exist, and gradually, through time, these elements change, thereby creating different organizational needs and demands. The imperative for the organization is to align itself with these changes.

In this view a manager's task is to understand the environmental changes that take place and to help the organization adapt to the new demands of the environment. Instead of taking for granted that managers have the capacity to reconfigure organizational goals with little regard to external constituencies, proponents of an ecological approach believe managers must be aware of changes in the environment and purposefully alter organizational processes and goals. Instead of focusing on internally oriented organizational goals and objectives, the organizational manager looks outward, into the world, to determine what is taking place and how the organization must adapt. A manager faces real problems that have real solutions. The failure to find the "right" solution most often relates directly to the failure of the organization to understand the environment or to successfully adapt itself to the demands "out there."

The implications of such a view for the world of higher education have been clearly shown over the last decade. Countless colleges and universities have perceived the decline in enrollment of the traditional age group as an objective demographic fact. The challenge for higher education institutions has been to understand the change in their markets, to create a new clientele, and to change themselves to meet the new demands of the environment.

Thus, a Catholic liberal arts college that primarily relied on local, upper-class Catholic families to send it their 18-year-old daughters adapted to the environment by broadening its market to include lower- and middle-income men and women, a wide array of religious denominations, and nontraditional students (Tierney, 1988b).

The consequences of an adaptive approach effect changes throughout the system. Students with different backgrounds often demand different kinds of curricular structures and different forms of student services. Indeed, for a Catholic college like the one just mentioned, environmental adaptation often entails, either explicitly or implicitly, a full-scale change of the organization's saga and culture.

The Enacted Environment

A wealth of research addresses how organizations construct (and destroy) organizational assumptions, premises, and goals (Gray, Bougon, & Donnellon, 1985; Gray & Staber, 1986; Morgan, 1980). Pfeffer (1981), Pondy (1978), Smircich and Morgan (1982), and Tierney (1987) have considered how leaders define and interpret organizational meaning; Nystrom and Starbuck (1984) have discussed the need to reinterpret the organizational universe consistently to avoid crises; and Deal (1984) has written about the symbolic, interpretive aspects of organizational change.

Smircich and Stubbart (1985) and Weick (1979) have provided a variety of strategies that concern the "enactment" of the external environment. "Boundaries between organizations and environment are never quite as clear-cut or stable as many organizational theorists think," notes Weick. "These boundaries shift, disappear, and are arbitrarily drawn" (p. 133). This approach thus assumes that organizational members create their own environments.

The underlying thesis of this perspective parallels the interest in organizational culture in higher education (Dill 1982; Masland, 1985; Tierney, 1988a). The assumption is that participants develop interpretations about the nature of the organization from their social construction of the organization's culture based on historical traditions, current situational contexts, and individual perceptions. The organization's culture focuses the participants' understanding of the environment by supplying many patterns and meanings.

The objectivist assumes that the environment is a comprehensive, objective, intractable set of facts. The organizational universe consists of a finite set of knowable elements. In contrast, enacted environments include any facts that come to the organization's attention, but exclude facts that do not. These environments view the world as more than a conscious set of demographic data and figures; the organization's understanding of the environment is not merely the sum of its parts. The organization has immense capacity, in this view, to create its environment through selective attention and interpretation.

Theorists of the enacted environment assume that an organization's culture comprises such a range of human experience that it is impossible to reduce meaning to predefined elements or to predictive value. Intentionality depends on the prior existence of a shared world of meaning within which organizational participants constitute their identities. Higher education organizations exist in socially constructed systems. They can neither be shielded from external interference and studied in a scientifically controlled environment, nor can they assume that the environment exists as a reified object. The social scientist's ability to comprehend events and the manager's ability to act begin with cultural definitions. All social science and administrative action exists in a cultural world, amid a web of signification we ourselves have spun (Geertz, 1973, p. 5).

Reality is not something objective or external to the participants. Instead, participant reality is defined through a process of social interchange in which perceptions are affirmed, modified, or replaced according to their apparent congruence with the perceptions of others. Rather than a biological or ecological model, the model of the enacted environment is based on a social construction of reality (Berger & Luckmann, 1967).

Such an interpretation has far-ranging consequences for higher education. Faced with declining enrollments in a traditional market, for example, administrators will not necessarily adapt to the environment. While they may note a business community's call for particular forms of occupational training, they will not interpret such a call as a curricular imperative. Instead, colleges will interpret their environments in unique and creative ways depending upon their individual cultures. The role of the college president in understanding and interpreting the environment to different constituencies becomes increasingly important. In particular, how leaders communicate and interpret institutional goals and values focuses the participants' comprehension of the environment.

Do leaders, for example, view the organization's relationship to their environment as one of dominance, weakness, or selectivity? Does a public state college view its audience in terms of its institutional saga or as a market to be "captured"?

How leaders and their participants respond to such questions helps explain why similar organizations use different decision-making strategies. One public state college, for example, will continue to cater to the needs of the local working class, whereas another will extend its geographical parameters as far as it takes to garner a new audience.

By noting that organizations not only respond to, but also help define, their environment through selective attention and interpretation, we observe once again that organizations are less social fact and more ongoing social definition. And such social definitions will have critical institutional consequences. The public state institution that extends its geographical boundaries and redefines its environment will also have to restructure its curriculum and student services. The institution that interprets its environment in terms of a "town-gown" antagonism will affect how the institution goes about its fundraising.

Implications of Enacted Environments for Researchers

Although it is helpful to understand both objectivist and enacted conceptions for research and practice, it is important to note that ideal versions of either approach rarely exist, and that most endeavors occur along a broad continuum. Nevertheless, administrators and researchers are accustomed to the traditional portion of the continuum. Most research in higher education has occurred within the boundaries of the objectivist paradigm, and most researchers and administrators still adhere to these assumptions. Over the past several decades, however, considerable activity has occurred on the other side of this continuum.

The shift in perspective from studying environments as objective facts to investigating environments as interpretive phenomena parallels a widespread movement in the social sciences and the humanities (Morgan & Smircich, 1980). The shift, often referred to as the "interpretive turn" (Rabinow &

Sullivan, 1979), finds researchers developing an alternative way to study social behavior and events. Researchers have replaced positivist research with
a concern for how we discern and interpret social reality. Peterson (1985)
characterizes the new, interpretive paradigm as one that studies "organizational elements as those that are subjective and must be interpreted, primarily by the organizational actors themselves" (p. 9).

Rather than isolating variables like the environment, or such environmental components as a particular market, interpretive researchers investigate various coexisting connections in an organization. That is, the researcher
tends to employ a holistic research design and analysis that emphasizes the
"cultural web of meaning" of the organization. To isolate a study of the environment from its organizational context belies the assumptions of the interpretive approach. An objectivist, for example, may find it appropriate to
conduct a study of an institution's changing demography. The approach argued for here, however, necessarily would begin an investigation by struggling to uncover how the organizational participants understand and
construct their reality and, within that reality, how they perceive the environment. What follows are three central components of an interpretive research design:

1. *An exploration of the multiple perceptions at work within the organization.* An organization's culture—the shared values, practices, and
symbols that constitute an organization—does not speak with one
voice. It is always cacophonous and multivocal. It is the researcher's
difficult job to uncover and interpret the multiple perspectives of organizational life.

Further, the researcher "seeks to understand the [participants']
thoughts and actions at a personal level, not at the far removed level
of abstract, aggregate statistics" (Smircich & Stubbart, 1985, p. 733).
This cannot be done solely through quantitative surveys or armchair
research, but only through intimate daily contact with institutional
life.

The guiding principle of the research is to construct a multifac-
eted approach to the study of organizations. Researchers do not enter
the field with preconceived notions about the problem to be studied
but, instead, attempt to understand the problem "from the natives'
point of view" (Geertz, 1983, p. 55). Researchers do not set out to

prove hypotheses, but, instead, enter the field with a theoretical framework based on the assumption that organizations are socially constructed.

In general, qualitative methods lie at the heart of the research design, although quantitative techniques can be employed to confirm, modify, or extend qualitative data. Detailed interviews following multiple formats are supplemented by a variety of qualitative methods. Structured interviews, open-ended interviews, follow-up sessions where specific questions are raised that relate to initial findings, and interviews that seek to confirm perceptual evidence provide formats for research interviews. Follow-up interviews allow researchers to recheck the validity of their initial findings and enable the interviewees to add data they may have omitted during the initial interview.

Participant observation in a variety of settings provides additional data. In addition, the researcher tries to uncover informational data such as language habits, forms and patterns of written communication, and the agendas and interaction at various kinds of meetings. Clues of particular interest concern how members of an institution interpret the school's history and environment both to themselves and to others.

2. *Longitudinal and historical analyses.* Researchers try to avoid a one-time snapshot of an institution; rather, they emphasize a longitudinal analysis. They place events and people into a historical context. Their research extends over time so they can determine how change occurs with regard to the research problem as well as its relationship to other organizational components. That is, the interpretive model assumes that present actions are linked not only to past events, but also to internal and external demands and shifts.

For a portrait of an organization to have any meaning, it must be fleshed out, detailed in description and rich in nuance. Interpretive research is best conducted when researchers observe a full cycle of organizational time. In the case of higher education institutions, that means an academic year at an institution. Periodic return visits to the institution or an intensive on-site study provide the researcher with an understanding of the research problem as it develops and changes over time.

3. *Institutional portraits.* Because colleges and universities are not two-dimensional, but are complex, highly interrelated collections of people, researchers provide their readers with ethnographic portraits and thick description (Geertz, 1973). Data presentation of this kind is consistent with recognized anthropological and sociological methods but is in many respects new to higher educational research. Instead of merely reporting incidents to the reader, the researcher involves the reader more fully in interpreting the data. The researcher wants the reader to step into the researcher's place and know the institution so well that the reader can interpret the data and reflect on the researcher's observations and conclusions. Rather than give the reader information, the researcher presents quotes and institutional portraits that show the organization's culture at work.

Hence, honest portraits of institutional life necessarily encompass the full range of human activity—from the courageous to the mundane. The researcher's observations often represent a highly candid portrait collectively drawn by institutional members. Studies of organizations need to move away from inaccurate portrayals of individuals as heroes or of static roles inhabited by powerless functionaries.

The approach called for here neither denies the worth of objectivist research nor refutes the need for multiple epistemological research perspectives. Indeed, different problems demand different research designs. Interpretive research yields different analyses and insights than the objectivist viewpoint. Alternative interpretations of research problems will provide useful insights about the problems and puzzles of higher education research.

Implications of Enacted Environments for Administrators

What are the implications for administrators in higher education if they view their organizational environment as enacted? I offer four proposals to higher education leaders: (1) find internal contradictions; (2) clarify the identity of the institution; (3) act on multiple, changing fronts; and (4) communicate. These suggestions are components of a diagnostic frame of reference, a way of living in the collegiate managerial environment. They are ways for administrators to identify what they need to do and how they need to do it, given the unique organization in which they find themselves.

Essentially, my point is that in part we need to reconceptualize the role of the higher education manager. The objectivist assumes that a strategic administrator must gather data "out there" and that a successful, unitary understanding of the environment exists. On the other hand, the interpretive assumption is that a strategic manager's task is "an imaginative one, a creative one, an art. . . . People make sense of their situation by engaging in an interpretive process that forms the basis for their organizational behavior" (Smircich & Stubbart, 1985, p. 730). The higher education administrator, then, cannot deal with the environment without dealing with the organization. Managers provide a vision and interpretation of the organization, and hence the environment, to organizational participants.

My hypothesis is that leaders are catalysts for perceptual change more than for physical change. I assume that environmental change is not linear and predictable and that it has complex, often spontaneous, ramifications. I will outline here four important leader behaviors, but the state of the art is too primitive to permit me to assert their sequence or their relative importance.

Find Internal Contradictions

Contradictions between what we do and what we say are often incongruities between the culture of the organization and the enacted environment. For example, some colleges recruit adult students but offer few evening courses and do not provide night registration, night services for students, or child care. Similarly, a college may say that it takes pride in the teaching skills of its faculty, but the road to tenure is paved with research publications.

Contradictions alert leaders to potential sources of future difficulties and identify areas where desired change has been implemented only partially. Contradictions reveal where additional efforts are needed to enhance widespread understanding of institutional purpose or direction. The search for contradictions tests whether the far-reaching ramifications of a proposed change will be as desirable as the expected local or short-term effects. One reason this simple activity has so much power is that it runs counter to our natural inclination to make orderly sense of our experiences, often by minimizing or ignoring contradictory evidence.

Clarify the Identity of the Institution

Identity begins with mission but goes beyond it to include vestiges of history and traces of the personalities of many current organizational participants.

Organizational identity includes certain capacities that are inherent in how participants arrange resources and the configuration of values, structure, and environment. Identity contains all elements that define what the organization is and suggests what it could become.

The mission expresses core values, many of which are similar among all higher education organizations. The importance of developing students' intellectual abilities is a value that all institutions of higher education share. Other elements of institutional mission tend to be common to a particular type such as religious colleges or public state institutions. Providing access and opportunity for "forgotten" students characterizes public state colleges, and religious institutions often have an expressed commitment to fostering values.

A strong sense of identity serves two important purposes: it fosters cultural integration, and it directs organizational action. In effect, it ensures that everyone is in the same boat and that they know where the boat is headed. Just as an international visitor tends to see a strange culture as incomprehensible, requiring him or her to expend great effort to function effectively, the organizational member in an inchoate culture lacks a regularized backdrop and guiding principles for his or her activities. Identity provides the framework for participants to deal with existential issues of their own worth and meaning in the organization.

Because new people join the institution every year and the institution changes constantly, a strong sense of identity must be cultivated, tended, and frequently revised. The institution needs an identity with roots in institutional history, but it also needs one that relates specifically to current conditions. A dynamic sense of identity allows the institution to choose and reject choices thrust on it by the environment. Rather than allowing the environment to determine organizational choice, to a certain extent, the institution is in charge of its destiny if it understands itself.

Act on Multiple, Changing Fronts

Foster activity in many areas of the organization. One year that might mean focusing on recruiting, student services, fund-raising, and board development; the next year it might be promotion policies, the classics department, management information systems, and financial aid. Here are some guidelines for approaching such activities:

1. *Treat every problem as if it had multiple solutions.* Organizations typically search only in the neighborhood of the problem and only until an acceptable solution materializes. Instead, search for multiple solutions until the best possible solution is found.

2. *Treat every solution as fleeting.* When environmental conditions change, yesterday's solution can easily become part of today's problem. But solutions get reified in many ways. The idea champion who received credit for a solution may be emotionally attached to it. Successful organizations do not eject current practice on a whim, but they are prepared to consider the possibility that the former solution is part of a major new problem.

3. *Look for consequences in unlikely places.* We might not expect devotion to accomplishing the university's goals to undermine faculty morale, but numerous examples exist where exactly such a problem occurred. Leaders who think through the possible ramifications of their actions are in a better position to choose and, having chosen, to recognize and ameliorate any undesired consequences.

4. *Beware of any solution that undermines strong values.* Solutions that undermine strong values will be resisted, perhaps rendering them unfeasible after all. They can be tempting, however, when it seems necessary to send a message to a truculent group or establish a major new institutional direction because of impinging environmental concerns. To advise caution is not to say that times exist when such moves are necessary. Recognizing the special difficulties that accompany radical cultural changes can prepare administrators to successfully carry them out.

Communicate

Members have only one way of understanding the organization's identity—through communication. They listen to speeches and read policy manuals; they also receive messages from behavior, events, and the minutiae of daily life. Individuals need to see and hear their leaders to be able to understand the environment. Convey a tangible, cohesive point of view about organizational life and the environment. Place equal emphasis on process and outcomes so that participants understand the consequences of implementing a decision as well as the content on the decision.

Use high levels of communication to convey messages about what the organization is, what is happening within and around it, and where it aims to go. Previous research (Baird, 1977) has found that several different organizational channels should be used for effective communication. Optimally, a mixture of written and oral messages, formal and informal networks, and hierarchical and lateral channels is needed before participants fully comprehend the organization and their role in it.

Conclusion

This chapter has advocated an alternative way of seeing and, hence, of acting in the organizational world. Rather than assuming we exist in an ecological universe where one's collegiate species must continually adapt, I argue that organizations and environments are socially constructed. I neither advocate nor believe that perception is always reality, yet I give credence to the idea that participants' perceptions of problems, solutions, the environment, and a host of other variables go a long way toward determining the health of the organization.

To be sure, budgets must be balanced, classrooms filled with students, and faculty paid. Yet, how we perceive that a budget should be balanced, who should sit in classrooms, what students should learn, and who should teach, depends in large part on the organization's enactment of its environment. By working within the framework of organizational culture, administrators learn to consider how change in one programmatic area will affect other areas. For example, rather than implement an open admissions policy to increase enrollment, the administrator will adopt a mode of strategic analysis that considers how such a change will affect the identity and inner workings of the college for both the short and long term.

The organizational researcher will forgo both predictive models of what the environment will look like in the future and causal solutions that view the environment in a deterministic manner. Instead, the researcher will provide "thick descriptions" of institutional perceptions of the environment and the decision-making consequences of those perceptions. Longitudinal studies will replace snapshots to determine how institutions change over time and the long-term effects of a decision.

To adopt the stance advocated here does not imply that organizations are anarchies where one decision is as good as another. Indeed, one implication of this chapter is that decisions do matter, but the route to making a decision does not lie with perfect information based on rational, instrumental facts and figures. Managers and researchers will gain additional insights if they view their organizations as unique cultures in dynamic environments and proceed from the notion that our interpretation of environmental change occurs in large part through the organizational participants' construction of the environment.

References

Baird, J. (1977). *The dynamics of organizational communication.* New York: Harper and Row.

Berger, P., & Luckmann, T. (1967). *The social construction of reality.* New York: Anchor.

Cameron, K. (1984). Organizational adaptation and higher education. *Journal of Higher Education, 55*(2), 122–144.

Chaffee, E. (1985). Three models of strategy. *Academy of Management Review, 20,* 89–98.

Chaffee, E., & Tierney, W. (1988). *Collegiate culture and leadership strategies.* New York: Macmillan.

Clark, B. (1971). Belief and loyalty in college organization. *Journal of Higher Education, 42*(6), 499–520.

Deal, T. (1984). Educational change: Revival tent, tinker toys, jungle, or carnival? *Teachers' College Record, 86,* 125–137.

Dill, D. (1982). The management of academic culture: Notes on the management of meaning and social integration. *Higher Education, 11,* 303–320.

Geertz, C. (1973). *The interpretation of culture.* New York: Basic Books.

Geertz, C. (1983). *Local knowledge.* New York: Basic Books.

Gray, B., Bougon, M., & Donnellon, A. (1985). Organizations as constructions and destructions of meaning. *Journal of Management, 11,* 83–98.

Gray, B., & Staber, U. (1986). *The destruction of meaning and the reshaping of organizational culture.* Unpublished manuscript.

Masland, A. (1985). Organizational culture in the study of higher education. *Review of Higher Education, 8,* 157–168.

Morgan, G. (1980). Paradigms, metaphors, and puzzle solving in organization theory. *Administrative Science Quarterly, 25,* 605–622.

Morgan, G., & Smircich, L. (1980). The case for qualitative research. *Administrative Science Quarterly, 5,* 491–500.

Nystrom, P., & Starbuck, W. (1984). To avoid organizational crises, unlearn. *Organizational Dynamics, 12,* 53–65.

Peterson, M. (1985). Emerging developments in postsecondary organization theory and research: Fragmentation or integration. *Educational Research, 14*, 5–12.

Pfeffer, J. (1981). Management as symbolic action: The creation and maintenance of organizational paradigms. *Organizational Behavior, 3*, 1–52.

Pondy, L. (1978). Leadership is a language game. In M. McCall and M. Lombardo (Eds.), *Leadership: Where else can we go?* (pp. 87–99). Durham, NC: Duke University Press.

Rabinow, P., & Sullivan, W. (1979). The interpretive turn: Emergence of an approach. In P. Rabinow & W. Sullivan (Eds.), *Interpretive Social Science* (pp. 1–30). Berkeley: University of California Press.

Smircich, L., & Morgan, G. (1982). Leadership: The management of meaning. *Journal of Applied Behavioral Science, 18*, 257–273.

Smircich, L., & Stubbart, C. (1985). Strategic management in an enacted world. *Academy of Management Review, 10*, 724–736.

Tierney, W. (1987). The semiotic aspects of leadership: An ethnographic perspective. *American Journal of Semiotics, 5*(2), 233–250.

Tierney, W. (1988a). Organizational culture in higher education: Defining the essentials. *The Journal of Higher Education, 59*(1), 2–21.

Tierney, W. (1988b). *The web of leadership: The presidency in higher education.* Greenwich, CT: JAI Press.

Weick, K. (1979). *The social psychology of organizing.* Reading, MA: Addison-Wesley.

Whetten, D., & Cameron, K. (1985). Administrative effectiveness in higher education. *Review of Higher Education, 9*, 35–49.

3

ORGANIZATIONAL CULTURE IN HIGHER EDUCATION

Defining the Essentials

Within the business community in the 1980s, organizational culture emerged as a topic of central concern to those who study organizations. Books such as Peters and Waterman's (1982) *In Search of Excellence*, Ouchi's (1983) *Theory Z*, Deal and Kennedy's (1982) *Corporate Cultures*, and Schein's (1985) *Organizational Culture and Leadership* emerged as major works in the study of managerial and organizational performance.

However, growing popular interest and research activity in organizational culture came as something of a mixed blessing. Heightened awareness brought with it increasingly broad and divergent concepts of culture. Researchers and practitioners alike often view culture as a new management approach that will not only cure a variety of organizational ills but will also serve to explain virtually every event that occurs within an organization. Moreover, widely varying definitions, research methods, and standards for understanding culture create confusion as often as they provide insight.

The intent of this chapter is neither to suggest that an understanding of organizational culture is an antidote for all administrative folly nor to imply that the surfeit of definitions of organizational culture makes its study meaningless for higher education administrators and researchers. Rather, the design of this chapter is to provide a working framework to diagnose culture in colleges and universities so that distinct problems can be overcome. The

This chapter originally appeared as Tierney, W. G. (1988). Organizational culture in higher education: Defining the essentials. *The Journal of Higher Education*, *59*(1), 2–21.

concepts for the framework come from a yearlong investigation of organizational culture in American higher education.

First, I provide a rationale for why organizational culture is a useful concept for understanding management and performance in higher education. In so doing, I point out how administrators might utilize the concept of culture to help solve specific administrative problems. The second part of the chapter considers previous attempts to define culture in organizations in general and, specifically, in colleges and universities. Third, a case study of a public state college highlights essential elements of academic culture. The conclusion explores possible avenues researchers might examine to enhance a usable framework of organizational culture for managers and researchers in higher education.

The Role of Culture in Management and Performance

Even the most seasoned college and university administrators often ask themselves, "What holds this place together? Is it mission, values, bureaucratic procedures, or strong personalities? How does this place run and what does it expect from its leaders?" These questions usually are asked in moments of frustration, when seemingly rational, well-laid plans have failed or have met with unexpected resistance. Similar questions are also asked frequently by members new to the organization, persons who want to know "how things are done around here." Questions like these seem difficult to answer because there is no one-to-one correspondence between actions and results. The same leadership style can easily produce widely divergent results in two ostensibly similar institutions. Likewise, institutions with very similar missions and curricula can perform quite differently because of the way their identities are communicated to internal and external constituents and because of the varying perceptions these groups may hold.

Institutions certainly are influenced by powerful, external factors such as demographic, economic, and political conditions, yet they are also shaped by strong forces that emanate from within. This internal dynamic has its roots in the history of the organization and derives its force from the values, processes, and goals held by those most intimately involved in the organization's workings. An organization's culture is reflected in what is done, how it is done, and who is involved in doing it. It concerns decisions, actions, and communication on both an instrumental and a symbolic level.

The anthropologist, Clifford Geertz (1973), writes that traditional culture "denotes a historically transmitted pattern of meanings embodied in symbols, a system of inherited conceptions expressed in symbolic forms by means of which [people] communicate, perpetuate, and develop their knowledge about and attitudes toward life" (p. 89). Organizational culture exists, then, in part through the actors' interpretation of historical and symbolic forms. The culture of an organization is grounded in the shared assumptions of individuals participating in the organization. Often taken for granted by the actors themselves, these assumptions can be identified through stories, special language, norms, institutional ideology, and attitudes that emerge from individual and organizational behavior.

Geertz (1973) defines culture by writing, "Man is an animal suspended in webs of significance he himself has spun. I take culture to be those webs, and the analysis of it to be therefore not an experimental science in search of law, but an interpretive one in search of meaning" (p. 5). Thus, an analysis of organizational culture of a college or university occurs as if the institution were an interconnected web that cannot be understood unless one looks not only at the structure and natural laws of that web but also at the actors' interpretations of the web itself. Organizational culture, then, is the study of particular webs of significance within an organizational setting. That is, we look at an organization as a traditional anthropologist would study a particular village or clan.

However, not unlike traditional villagers, administrators often have only an intuitive grasp of the cultural conditions and influences that enter into their daily decision making. In this respect they are not unlike most of us who have a dim, passive awareness of cultural codes, symbols, and conventions that are at work in society at large. Only when we break these codes and conventions are we forcibly reminded of their presence and considerable power. Likewise, administrators tend to recognize their organization's culture only when they have transgressed its bounds and severe conflicts or adverse relationships ensue. As a result, we frequently find ourselves dealing with organizational culture in an atmosphere of crisis management, instead of reasoned reflection and consensual change.

Our lack of understanding about the role of organizational culture in improving management and institutional performance inhibits our ability to address the challenges that face higher education. As these challenges mount, our need to understand organizational culture only intensifies. Like many

American institutions, colleges and universities face increasing complexity and fragmentation.

As decision-making contexts grow more obscure, costs increase, and resources become more difficult to allocate, leaders in higher education can benefit from understanding their institutions as cultural entities. As before, these leaders continue to make difficult decisions. These decisions, however, need not engender the degree of conflict that they usually have prompted. Indeed, properly informed by an awareness of culture, tough decisions may contribute to an institution's sense of purpose and identity. Moreover, to implement decisions, leaders must have a full, nuanced understanding of the organization's culture. Only then can they articulate decisions in a way that will speak to the needs of various constituencies and marshal their support.

Cultural influences occur at many levels, within the department and the institution, as well as at the system and state level. Because these cultures can vary dramatically, a central goal of understanding organizational culture is to minimize the occurrence and consequences of cultural conflict and help foster the development of shared goals. Studying the cultural dynamics of educational institutions and systems equips us to understand and, one hopes, reduce adversarial relationships. Equally important, it will enable us to recognize how those actions and shared goals are most likely to succeed and how they can best be implemented. One assumption of this chapter is that more often than not more than one choice exists for the decision maker; one simple answer seldom occurs. No matter how much information we gather, we can often choose from several viable alternatives. Culture influences the decision.

Effective administrators are well aware that they can take a given action in some institutions but not in others. They are less aware of why this is true. Bringing the dimensions and dynamics of culture to consciousness will help leaders assess the reasons for such differences in institutional responsiveness and performance. This will allow them to evaluate likely consequences before, not after, they act.

It is important to reiterate that an understanding of organizational culture is not a panacea for all administrative problems. An understanding of culture, for example, will not automatically increase enrollments or fundraising. However, an administrator's correct interpretation of the organization's culture can provide critical insight about which of many possible avenues to choose in reaching a decision about how to increase enrollment or undertake a particular approach to a fund-raising campaign. Indeed, the most persuasive case for studying organizational culture is quite simply that we no longer need to tolerate the consequences of our ignorance, nor, for that matter, will a rapidly changing environment permit us to do so.

By advocating a broad perspective, organizational culture encourages practitioners to

- consider real or potential conflicts, not in isolation, but on the broad canvas of organizational life;
- recognize structural or operational contradictions that suggest tensions in the organization;
- implement and evaluate everyday decisions with a keen awareness of their role in and influence on organizational culture;
- understand the symbolic dimensions of ostensibly instrumental decisions and actions; and
- consider why different groups in the organization have varying perceptions about institutional performance.

Many administrators intuitively understand that organizational culture is important, and their actions sometimes reflect the points just mentioned. A framework for organizational culture will provide administrators with the capacity to better articulate and address this crucial foundation for improving performance.

Thus far, however, a usable definition of organizational culture appropriate to higher education has remained elusive. If we are to enable administrators and policy makers to implement effective strategies within their own cultures, then we must first understand a culture's structure and components. A provisional framework will lend the concept of culture definitional rigor so that practitioners can analyze their own cultures and ultimately improve the performance of their organizations and systems. The understanding of culture will thus aid administrators in spotting and resolving potential conflicts and in managing change more effectively and efficiently. However, if we are to enable administrators and researchers to implement effective strategies within their own cultures, then we first must make explicit the essential elements of culture.

Cultural Research: Where Have We Been

Organizations as Cultures

Ouchi and Wilkins (1985) note: "Few readers would disagree that the study of organizational culture has become one of the major domains of organizational research, and some might even argue that it has become the single most active arena, eclipsing studies of formal structure, of organization-environment research and of bureaucracy" (pp. 457–458).

Researchers have examined institutions, organizations, and subunits of organization as distinct and separate cultures with unique sets of ceremonies, rites, and traditions (Mitroff & Kilmann, 1976; Morgan, Frost, & Pondy, 1983; Pettigrew, 1979; Trice & Beyer, 1984), and initial attempts have been made to analyze leadership from a cultural perspective (Bennis, 1984; Pfeffer, 1981; Schein, 1983; Smircich & Morgan, 1982). The role of cultural communication has been examined by March (1984), Feldman and March (1981), Putnam and Pacanowsky (1983), Trujillo (1983), Tierney (1985), and Pondy (1978). Organizational stories and symbols have also been investigated (Dandridge, 1985; Dandridge, Mitroff, & Joyce, 1980; Mitroff & Kilmann, 1975; Tierney, 1987).

Findings indicate that strong, congruent cultures supportive of organizational structures and strategies are more effective than weak, incongruent, or disconnected cultures (Cameron, 1987; Krakower, 1985). Moreover, the work of numerous theorists (Burrell & Morgan, 1979; Koprowski, 1983; Mitroff & Mason, 1982; Quinn & Rohrbaugh, 1981) suggests that there is an identifiable deep structure and set of core assumptions that may be used to examine and understand culture.

Colleges and Universities as Cultures

Numerous writers (e.g., Chait, 1982; Dill, 1982) have noted the lack of cultural research in higher education. Dill has commented: "Ironically the organizations in Western society which most approximate the essential characteristics of Japanese firms are academic institutions. They are characterized by lifetime employment, collective decision making, individual responsibility, infrequent promotion, and implicit, informal evaluation" (p. 307). Research in higher education, however, has moved toward defining managerial techniques based on strategic planning, marketing, and management control.

Higher education researchers have made some attempts to study campus cultures. Initially, in the early 1960s, the study of culture primarily concerned student cultures (Becker, 1963; Bushnell, 1960; Clark, 1963; Davie & Hare, 1956; Pace, 1960, 1962). Clark pioneered work on distinctive colleges as cultures (1970), the role of belief and loyalty in college organizations (1971), and organizational sagas as tools for institutional identity (1972). Work in the 1980s included the study of academic cultures (Becher, 1981; Freedman, 1979; Gaff & Wilson, 1971); leadership (Chaffee, 1984; Chaffee & Tierney, 1988; Tierney, 1988); and the system of higher education as a culture (Bourdieu, 1977; Clark, 1984). Thus, a foundation has been prepared on which we can build a framework for studying culture in higher education.

A Cultural Framework: Where We Might Go

Anthropologists enter the field with an understanding of such cultural terms as "kinship" or "lineage." Likewise, productive research depends on our being able to enter the field armed with equally well-defined concepts. These terms provide clues for uncovering aspects of organizational culture as they also define elements of a usable framework. Necessarily then, we need to consider what cultural concepts can be used by cultural researchers when they study a college or university. This chapter provides an initial attempt to identify the operative cultural concepts and terms in collegiate institutions.

Identification of the concepts was developed through analysis of a case study of one institution. By delineating and describing key dimensions of culture, I do not presume to imply that all institutions are culturally alike. The intense analysis of one institution provides a more specific understanding of organizational culture than we presently have and presumably will enable researchers to expand upon the framework presented here.

Of the many possible avenues for the cultural researcher to investigate, Table 3.1 outlines essential concepts to be studied at a college or university. That is, if an anthropologist conducted an in-depth ethnography at a college or university and omitted any mention of institutional mission, we would note that the anthropologist had overlooked an important cultural term.

Each cultural term occurs in organizational settings, yet the way it occurs, the form it takes, and the importance it has differs dramatically. One college, for example, might have a history of formal, autocratic leadership,

TABLE 3.1
A Framework of Organizational Culture

Environment:
- How does the organization define its environment?
- What is the attitude toward the environment? (Hostility? Friendship?)

Mission:
- How is it defined?
- How is it articulated?
- Is it used as a basis for decisions?
- How much agreement is there?

Socialization:
- How do new members become socialized?
- How is it articulated?
- What do we need to know to survive/excel in this organization?

Information:
- What constitutes information?
- Who has it?
- How is it disseminated?

Strategy:
- How are decisions arrived at?
- Which strategy is used?
- Who makes decisions?
- What is the penalty for bad decisions?

Leadership:
- What does the organization expect from its leaders?
- Who are the leaders?
- Are there formal and informal leaders?

---

whereas another institution might operate with an informal, consensually oriented leader. To illustrate the meaning of each term, I provide examples drawn from a case study of a public institution identified here as "Family State College." The data are drawn from site visits conducted during the 1984–85 academic year. Participant observation and interviews with a random sample of the entire college community lend *thick description* (Geertz, 1973) to the analysis, and each example highlights representative findings of the college community.

Family State College

Writes David Dill (1982):

> The intensity of an academic culture is determined not only by the richness
> and relevance of its symbolism for the maintenance of the professional
> craft, but by the bonds of social organization. For this mechanism to oper-
> ate, the institution needs to take specific steps to socialize the individual to
> the belief system of the organization. . . . The management of academic
> culture therefore involves both the management of meaning and the man-
> agement of social integration. (p. 317)

Family State College offers insight into a strong organizational culture
and exemplifies how administrators at this campus use the "management of
meaning" to foster understanding of the institution and motivate support
for its mission.

In dealing with its environment, Family State College has imbued in its
constituents a strong feeling that the institution has a distinctive purpose and
that its programs reflect its mission. By invigorating old roots and values
with new meaning and purpose, the president of Family State has largely
succeeded in reconstructing tradition and encouraging a more effective organizational culture. As with all executive action, however, the utilization,
strengths, and weaknesses of a particular approach are circumscribed by institutional context.

Environment

Founded in 1894, Family State College exists in a fading industrial town.
The institution has always been a career-oriented college for the working
class in nearby towns and throughout the state. "I came here," related one
student, "because I couldn't afford going to another school, and it was real
close by." Fifty percent of the students remain in the local area after graduation, and an even higher percentage (80%) reside in the state. In many respects the city of Family and the surrounding area have remained a relatively
stable environment for the state college because of the unchanging nature of
the working-class neighborhoods. An industrial arts professor explained the
town-gown relationship: "The college has always been for the people here.
This is the type of place that was the last stop for a lot of kids. They are

generally the first generation to go to college, and college for them has always meant getting a job."

When Family State's president arrived in 1976, he inherited an institution in equilibrium yet with a clear potential to become stagnant. The institution had low visibility in the area and next to no political clout in the state capital. Family State was not a turbulent campus in the late 1970s; rather, it was a complacent institution without a clear direction. In the past decade the institutional climate has changed from complacency to excitement, and constituents share a desire to improve the college.

The college environment provided rationales for change. Dwindling demand for teachers required that the college restructure its teacher-education program. A statewide tax that eliminated "nonessential" programs in high schools reduced the demand for industrial arts at Family State. New requirements by state hospitals brought about a restructured medical technology program. The college's relationship to its environment fostered a close identification with its working-class constituency and prompted change based on the needs of a particular clientele.

Mission

Individuals spoke of the mission of the college from one of two angles: the mission referred either to the balance between career-oriented and liberal arts programs or to the audience for whom the college had been founded—the working class. Although people spoke about the mission of the college in terms of both program and clientele, the college's adaptations concerned programmatic change, not a shift in audience. That is, in 1965, the college created a nursing program that easily fit into the mission of the college as a course of study for working-class students. An industrial technology major is another example of a program that responded to the needs of the surrounding environment and catered to the specific mission of the institution. Rather than alter or broaden the traditional constituency of the institution, the college tried to create new curricular models that would continue to attract the working-class student to Family State.

As a consequence, the college continues to orient itself to its traditional clientele—the working people of the area. The city and the surrounding area have remained a working-class region throughout the college's history; the town has neither prospered and become middle class, nor has it faded into oblivion. Continuing education programs and the courtship of adult learners have broadened the clientele of the college while maintaining its traditional, working-class constituency.

The president frequently articulates his vision of the institutional mission in his speeches and writing. One individual commented: "When I first came here and the president said that 'we're number one' I just thought it was something he said, like every college president says. But after [you're here] awhile you watch the guy and you see he really believes it. So I believe it too." "We are number one in a lot of programs," said the president. "We'll go head-to-head with a lot of other institutions. Our programs in nursing, communication, and industrial technology can stack up against any other state college here. I'd say we're the best institution of this kind in the state."

Presidential pronouncements of excellence and the clear articulation of institutional mission have a twofold import: First, institutional mission provides the rationale and criteria for the development of a cohesive curricular program. Second, the president and the other organizational participants have a standard for self-criticism and performance. All too often, words such as "excellence" can be so vague that they have no measurable meaning. Family State however, can "stack up against any other state college." That is, rather than criterion-referenced performance measures such as standardized tests and achievement levels of incoming students, Family State College has standards of excellence that are consistent with the historic mission of state colleges.

Socialization

One individual who had recently begun working at the college noted: "People smiled and said hello here. It was a friendly introduction. People said to me, 'Oh, you'll really love it here.' It was that wonderful personal touch. When they hire someone here, they don't want only someone who can do the job, but someone who will also fit in with the personality of the place." One individual also noted that, soon after he arrived, the president commented on how well he did his work but was worried that he wasn't "fitting in" with the rest of the staff. What makes these comments interesting is that they are about a public state college. Such institutions often have the reputation of being impersonal and bureaucratic, as opposed to having the "personal touch" of private colleges.

A student commented: "If a student hasn't gotten to know the president in a year, then it's the student's damn fault. Everybody sees him walking around here. He's got those Monday meetings. He comes to all the events. I mean, he's really easy to see if you've got something you want to talk to him about. That's what's special about Family. How many places can a student get to know the president? We all call him 'Danny' (not to his face) because he's so familiar to us." The student's comment is particularly telling in an era of declining enrollments. One reason students come to the school, and one reason they stay at Family, is because the entire institution reflects concern and care for students as personified by the president's open door and the easy accessibility of all administrators.

Information

People mentioned that all segments of the institution were available to one another to help solve problems. Every Monday afternoon the president held an open house where any member of the college community could enter his office and talk to him. All segments of the community used the vehicle. As one administrator reported: "That's sacred time. The president wants to know the problems of the different constituencies. People seem to use it. He reflects through the open house that he really cares."

The president also believes in the power of the written word, especially with respect to external constituencies. It is not uncommon to read about Family State or the president in the local press. A survey done by the college discovered that the local citizenry had a positive, working knowledge of the president and the college. The president attends a multitude of local functions, such as chamber of commerce and United Way meetings, and civic activities. He also invites the community onto the college campus.

Although mailings and written information are important vehicles for sharing information with external constituencies, oral discourse predominates among members of the institution. Internal constituencies appear well informed about decisions and ideas through an almost constant verbal exchange of information through both formal and informal means. Formal means of oral communication include task forces, executive council meetings, and college-wide activities. At these gatherings individuals not only share information but also discuss possible solutions to problems or alternatives to a particular dilemma.

The president's communicative style percolates throughout the institution. Information from top administrators is communicated to particular audiences through weekly meetings of individual departments. One vice president described the process: "The president's executive staff meets once a week, and we, in turn, meet with our own people. There's lots of give and take. The key around here is that we're involved in a process to better serve students. Open communication facilitates the process. God help the administrator or faculty member who doesn't work for students."

Informal channels of communication at Family State are an equally, if not more, important means for sharing and discussing ideas as well as developing an esprit de corps. The president hosts several functions each year at his house near campus. He brings together disparate segments of the college community, such as different faculty departments, for a casual get-together over supper, brunch, or cocktails. "This is like a family," explained the president. "Too often people don't have the time to get together and share with one another food and drink in a pleasant setting."

It is not uncommon to see many different segments of the institution gathered together in public meeting places such as the cafeteria or a lounge. In discussions with faculty, staff, and administrators, many people showed a working knowledge of one another's tasks and duties and, most strikingly, the student body.

Throughout the interviews individuals consistently mentioned the "family atmosphere" that had developed at the college. As one individual noted: "Everything used to be fragmented here. Now there's a closeness."

Strategy

Family State's decision-making process followed a formal sequence that nevertheless accommodated informal activity. Initiatives often began at the individual or departmental level, as with proposals to create a new program. Eventually the new program or concept ended up in the College Senate—composed of faculty, students, and administrators. A subcommittee of the senate decided what action should be taken and recommended that the idea be accepted or defeated. The senate then voted on the issue. Once it had taken action, the next step was presidential—accept the proposal, veto it, or send it back to the senate for more analysis. The final step was approval by the board.

Formalized structures notwithstanding, a strictly linear map of decision analysis would be misleading. Most often the administration made decisions by widespread discussion and dialogue. "It's participative decision making," commented one individual. The president's decisions existed in concrete, but individuals saw those decisions as building blocks upon which further, more participative decisions were made. "The key around here," observed one administrator, "is that we're involved in a process to better serve students. Open communication facilitates the process."

Although, as noted, the college has adapted to its environment, the college did not rely solely on adaptive strategy. The president noted: "I don't believe that an institution serves its culture well if it simply adapts. The marketplace is narrow and changes quickly." Instead, the administration, particularly the president, has brought about change through an interpretive strategy based on the strategic use of symbols in the college and surrounding environment.

Chaffee (1985) defines interpretive strategy as ways that organizational representatives "convey meanings that are intended to motivate stakeholders" (p. 941). Interpretive strategy orients metaphors or frames of reference that allow the organization and its environment to be understood by its constituents. Unlike strategic models that enable the organization to achieve goals or adapt to the environment, interpretive strategy proceeds from the understanding that the organization can play a role in creating its environment. Family State's president accentuates process, concern for the individual as a person, and the central orientation of serving students. He does so through several vehicles, foremost among them being communication with constituencies and the strategic use of space and time.

The president's use of space is an important element in his leadership style and strategy implementation. He frequently extends his spatial domain beyond the confines of the college campus into the city and surrounding towns. Conversely, invitations to the community to attend events at the college and use the library and other facilities have reduced spatial barriers with a city that otherwise might feel excluded. Informal gatherings, such as suppers at the president's house or luncheons at the college, have brought together diverse constituencies that otherwise have little reason to interact with one another. Moreover, the president has attended to the physical appearance of the institution, making it an effective symbol to his constituencies that even the grounds demand excellence and care.

The president's symbolic use of space sets an example emulated by others. His open-door policy, for example, permeates the institution. Administrators either work in open-space areas in full view of one another, or the doors to their offices are physically open, inviting visits with colleagues, guests, and, more important, students. The openness of the president's and other administrators' doors creates an informality throughout the college that fosters widespread sharing of information and an awareness of decisions and current activities.

The president is also a visible presence on the campus. He spends part of every day walking throughout the institution for a casual inspection of the grounds and facilities. These walks provide a way for people to talk with him about matters of general concern and enable him to note something that he may not have seen if he had not walked around the campus. Administrators, too, interact with one another and with students, not only in their offices, but on the other's "turf." "The atmosphere here is to get to know students," said one administrator, "see them where they are and not have a host of blockades so students feel as if they are not listened to."

Discussion of communication and space has made reference to time. The president continually integrates formal and informal interactions with his constituencies. According to the president's secretary and a study of the presidential calendar, about one and one-half hours per day are scheduled as "free time" that he uses as he sees fit—for reading, writing, or perhaps walking around the campus.

The president regularly schedules meetings with his executive circle or individuals such as the treasurer. The meetings revolve around both a mixture of formal agenda-like items and ideas or problems that either the president or his lieutenants feel they have. Although his schedule is generally very busy, it is not difficult to see the president. His secretary makes his appointments. She notes that if a faculty member or administrator asks to see the president, she would schedule an appointment when he was available in the very near future. Students, too, can see the president, but his secretary generally tries to act as a gatekeeper to ensure that the students really need to see the president and not someone else.

Leadership

The president's awareness of patterns and styles of communication and his conscious use of time and place are perhaps best illustrated by a meeting we had during one of our site visits to Family State. We waited in the president's outer office with the director of institutional research.

The door swung open, and the president walked out to greet us. He said,

I'm sorry for being late. I knew about your appointment and had planned to be back here on time, but I was walking around the campus for 45 minutes, and just at the last minute I made a detour to check out the cafeteria, to see how things were going. I met a guy down there who works in the kitchen, and he and I have always said we should play cribbage some time (he's a cribbage player), and wouldn't you know, he had a board with him today and he asked me to play. So I did. He beat me, too. So I wasn't doing anything very presidential in being late for you. I was just walking around the campus on this beautiful day, and playing cribbage in the kitchen with a friend.

The president's disclaimer notwithstanding, his actions are presidential in that they develop and reinforce an institutional culture. His effective use of symbols and frames of reference, both formally and informally, articulates the college's values and goals and helps garner support from faculty, students, staff, and the community. This should not imply, however, that presidents should necessarily spend their time walking around campus or playing cribbage with the kitchen help. What is effective at one institution is unlikely to work at another. Nevertheless, the role of symbolic communication that we witness on this campus, buttressed by tangible, constructive change, provides valuable clues about effectiveness and organizational culture.

Tying the Framework Together

People come to believe in their institution by the ways they interact and communicate with one another. The ongoing cultural norms of Family State foster an implicit belief in the mission of the college as providing a public good. In this sense, staff, faculty members, and administrators all feel they contribute to a common good—the education of working-class students. When individuals apply for work at Family State, they are considered not only on the basis of skill and qualifications but also on how they will fit into the cultural milieu. Socialization occurs rapidly through symbols such as open doors, the constant informal flow of communication punctuated by good-natured kidding, access throughout the organization, dedication to hard work, and, above all, commitment to excellence for students. When people speak of their mission, they speak of helping people. Members of the college community work from the assumption that an individual's actions do matter, can turn around a college, and can help alter society.

Belief in the institution emerges as all the more important, given an unstable economic and political environment. The district in which the college lies has little political clout, and consequently the institution is not politically secure. Rapidly shifting employment patterns necessarily demand that the institution have program flexibility. Although the college has created programs such as medical technology and communication/media, it has not made widespread use of adaptive strategy.

"The strength of academic culture," states David Dill (1982),

> is particularly important when academic institutions face declining resources. During these periods the social fabric of the community is under great strain. If the common academic culture has not been carefully nurtured during periods of prosperity, the result can be destructive conflicts between faculties, loss of professional morale, and personal alienation. (p. 304)

Family State College exemplifies a strong organizational culture. Further, the academic culture nurtures academic excellence and effectiveness.

It is important to reiterate, however, that all effective and efficient institutions will not have similar cultures. The leadership exhibited by the president at Family State, for example, would fail miserably at an institution with a different culture. Similarly, the role of mission at Family State would be inappropriate for different kinds of colleges and universities. The rationale for a cultural framework is not to presume that all organizations should function similarly, but rather to provide managers and researchers with a schema to diagnose their own organizations.

In providing a provisional framework for the reader, I have neither intended that we assume the different components of the cultural framework are static and mutually exclusive, nor that an understanding of organizational culture will solve all institutional dilemmas. If we return to the Geertzian notion of culture as an interconnected web of relationships, we observe that the components of culture will overlap and connect with one another. In the case study, for example, the way the leader articulated organizational mission spoke both to the saga of the institution and to its leadership.

How actors interpret the organizational "web" will not provide the right answers to simplistic choices. Rather, a cultural analysis empowers managers with information previously unavailable or implicit about their organization, which, in turn, can help solve critical organizational dilemmas. As with any decision-making strategy, all problems cannot be solved simply because an individual uses a particular focus on an issue. For example, a specific answer to whether tuition should be raised by a particular percentage obviously will not find a solution by understanding culture. On the other hand, what kind of clientele the institution should have or what its mission should be as it adapts to environmental change are critical issues that speak to the costs of tuition and demand cultural analysis.

Conclusion: Where Do We Go From Here?

Many possible avenues await the investigation of organizational culture. This chapter has provided merely the essential terms for the study of academic culture. A comprehensive study of organizational culture in academic settings will demand increased awareness of determinants such as individual and organizational use of time, space, and communication. In this case study, we observed the president's formal and informal uses of different cultural concepts. Individuals noted, for example, how they were well informed of administrative decisions and plans primarily through informal processes. Evidence such as the president's casual conversations with administrators or walking around the campus were effective examples of the informal use of time. Further work needs to be done concerning the meaning and effective use of formality and informality with regard to time, space, and communication.

I have used the term "organizational culture" but have made no mention of its subsets: subculture, anticulture, or disciplinary culture. An investigation of these cultural subsets will provide administrators with useful information about how to increase performance and decrease conflict in particular groups. We also must investigate the system of higher education to understand its impact on individual institutions. For example, state systems undoubtedly influence the culture of a public state college in ways other than budgetary. A study of the influence of states on institutional culture appears warranted.

Each term noted in Table 3.1 also demands further explication and analysis. Indeed, the concepts presented here are an initial attempt to establish a framework for describing and evaluating various dimensions of organizational culture. Developing such a framework is an iterative process that should benefit from the insights of further research endeavors. An important research activity for the future will be the refinement and extension of this framework. The methodological tools and skills for such cultural studies also need elaboration.

By developing this framework and improving ways of assessing organizational culture we will put administrators in a better position to change elements in the institution that are at variance with the culture. This research will permit them to effect orderly change in the organization without creating unnecessary conflict. Moreover, the continued refinement of this framework will permit research to become more cumulative and will help foster further collaborative efforts among researchers.

References

Becher, T. (1981). Toward a definition of disciplinary cultures. *Studies in Higher Education, 6,* 109–122.

Becker, H. S. (1963). Student culture. In T. F. Lunsford (Ed.), *The study of campus cultures* (pp. 11–26). Boulder, CO: Western Interstate Commission for Higher Education.

Bennis, W. (1984). Transformative power and leadership. In T. J. Sergiovanni & J. E. Corbally (Eds.), *Leadership and organizational culture* (pp. 64–71). Urbana: University of Illinois Press.

Bourdieu, P. (1977). Systems of education and systems of thought. *International Social Science Journal, 19,* 338–358.

Burrell, G., & Morgan, G. (1979). *Sociological paradigms and organizational analysis.* London: Heinemann.

Bushnell, J. (1960). Student values: A summary of research and future problems. In M. Carpenter (Ed.), *The larger learning* (pp. 45–61). Dubuque, IA: Brown.

Cameron, K. S. (1987). Measuring organizational effectiveness in institutions of higher education. *Administrative Science Quarterly, 23,* 604–632.

Chaffee, E. E. (1984). *After decline, what? Survival strategies at eight private colleges.* Boulder, CO: National Center for Higher Education Management Systems.

Chaffee, E. E. (1985). Three models of strategy. *Academy of Management Review, 10,* 89–98.

Chaffee, E. E., & Tierney, W. G. (1988). *Collegiate culture and leadership strategies.* New York: Macmillan.

Chait, R. P. (1982). Look who invented Japanese management! *AGB Quarterly, 17,* 3–7.

Clark, B. R. (1963). Faculty culture. In T. F. Lunsford (Ed.), *The study of campus cultures* (pp. 39–54). Boulder, CO: Western Interstate Commission for Higher Education.

Clark, B. R. (1970). *The distinctive college.* Chicago, IL: Aldine.

Clark, B. R. (1971). Belief and loyalty in college organization. *Journal of Higher Education, 42,* 499–520.

Clark, B. R. (1972). The organizational saga in higher education. *Administrative Science Quarterly, 17*(2), 178–184.

Clark, B. R. (Ed.). (1984). *Perspectives in higher education.* Berkeley: University of California Press.

Dandridge, T. C. (1985). The life stages of a symbol: When symbols work and when they can't. In P. J. Frost, L. F. Moore, M. R. Louis, C. C. Lundberg, & J. Martin (Eds.), *Organizational culture* (pp. 141–154). Beverly Hills, CA: Sage.

Dandridge, T. C., Mitroff, I., & Joyce, W. F. (1980). Organizational symbolism: A topic to expand organizational analysis. *Academy of Management Review, 5,* 77–82.

Davie, J. S., & Hare, A. P. (1956). Button-down collar culture. *Human Organization, 14,* 13–20.

Deal, T. E., & Kennedy, A. A. (1982). *Corporate cultures: The rites and rituals of corporate life.* Reading, MA: Addison-Wesley.

Dill, D. D. (1982). The management of academic culture: Notes on the management of meaning and social integration. *Higher Education, 11,* 303–320.

Feldman, M. S., & March, J. G. (1981). Information in organizations as signal and symbol. *Administrative Science Quarterly, 26,* 171–186.

Freedman, M. (1979). *Academic culture and faculty development.* Berkeley: University of California Press.

Gaff, J. G., & Wilson, R. C. (1971). Faculty cultures and interdisciplinary studies. *Journal of Higher Education, 42,* 186–201.

Geertz, C. (1973). *The interpretation of cultures.* New York: Basic Books.

Koprowski, E. J. (1983). Cultural myths: Clues to effective management. *Organizational Dynamics, 12*(2), 39–51.

Krakower, J. Y. (1985). *Assessing organizational effectiveness: Considerations and procedures.* Boulder, CO: National Center for Higher Education Management Systems.

March, J. G. (1984). How we talk and how we act: Administrative theory and administrative life. In T. J. Sergiovanni & J. E. Corbally (Eds.), *Leadership and organizational culture* (pp. 18–35). Urbana: University of Illinois Press.

Mitroff, I. I., & Kilmann, R. H. (1975). Stories managers tell: A new tool for organizational problem solving. *Management Review, 64,* 18–28.

Mitroff, I. I., & Kilmann, R. H. (1976). On organizational stories: An approach to the design and analysis of organizations through myths and stories. In R. H. Kilmann, L. R. Pondy, & D. P. Slevin (Eds.), *The management of organization design* (pp. 189–207). New York: North Holland.

Mitroff, I. I., & Mason, R. (1982). Business policy and metaphysics: Some philosophical considerations. *Academy of Management Review, 7*, 361–370.

Morgan, G., Frost, P. J., & Pondy, L. R. (1983). Organizational symbolism. In L. R. Pondy, P. J. Frost, & T. C. Dandridge (Eds.), *Organizational symbolism* (pp. 55–65). Greenwich, CT: JAI Press.

Ouchi, W. G. (1983). Theory Z: An elaboration of methodology and findings. *Journal of Contemporary Business, 11*, 27–41.

Ouchi, W. G., & Wilkins, A. L. (1985). Organizational culture. *Annual Review of Sociology, 11*, 457–483.

Pace, C. R. (1960). Five college environments. *College Board Review, 41*, 24–28.

Pace, C. R. (1962). Methods of describing college cultures. *Teachers College Record, 63*, 267–277.

Peters, T. J., & Waterman, R. H. (1982). *In search of excellence.* New York: Harper and Row.

Pettigrew, A. M. (1979). On studying organizational cultures. *Administrative Science Quarterly, 24*, 570–581.

Pfeffer, J. (1981). Management as symbolic action: The creation and maintenance of organizational paradigms. *Research in Organizational Behavior, 3*, 1–52.

Pondy, L. R. (1978). Leadership is a language game. In M. McCall & M. Lombardo (Eds.), *Leadership: Where else can we go?* (pp. 87–99). Durham, NC: Duke University Press.

Putnam, L. L., & Pacanowsky, M. E. (Eds.). (1983). *Communication and organizations: An interpretive approach.* Beverly Hills, CA: Sage.

Quinn, R. E., & Rohrbaugh, J. (1981). A competing values approach to organizational effectiveness. *Public Productivity Review, 5*, 122–140.

Schein, E. H. (1983). The role of the founder in creating organizational culture. *Organizational Dynamics, 12*, 13–28.

Schein, E. H. (1985). *Organizational culture and leadership.* San Francisco: Jossey-Bass.

Smircich, L., & Morgan, G. (1982). Leadership: The management of meaning. *Journal of Applied Behavioral Science, 18*, 257–273.

Tierney, W. G. (1985). The communication of leadership. Working paper. Boulder, CO: National Center for Higher Education Management Systems.

Tierney, W. G. (1987). The semiotic aspects of leadership: An ethnographic perspective. *American Journal of Semiotics, 5*(2), 233–250.

Tierney, W. G. (1988). *The web of leadership: The presidency in higher education.* Greenwich, CT: JAI Press.

Trice, H. M., & Beyer, J. M. (1984). Studying organizational cultures through rites and ceremonials. *Academy of Management Review, 9,* 653–669.

Trujillo, N. (1983). "Performing" Mintzberg's roles: The nature of managerial communication. In L. L. Putnam & M. E. Pacanowsky (Eds.), *Communication and organizations: An interpretive approach.* Beverly Hills, CA: Sage.

PART TWO

EXAMINING ACADEMIC LIFE

4

ACADEMIC WORK AND INSTITUTIONAL CULTURE
Constructing Knowledge

I t is early in the fall semester, and I am interviewing faculty, students, and parents at Christian University (a pseudonym), a 100-year-old urban institution with 3,000 students and 200 faculty. Christian is "on the move"; it has added a continuing education program and a graduate school, and it now serves a regional, rather than local, clientele.

Portrait of Christian University

The administration, faculty, and vast majority of the student body are evangelical Christians. A student explains: "Being a Christian in a public high school was tough. People made fun of me. I very much wanted a college that was dedicated to a Christian way of life. People acknowledge God here, so I don't have to defend myself. Christian University allowed me to find the truth, rather than push me into the corner."

Throughout the institution people speak of Christianity as the guiding principle for what they do. The president refers to the school's mission as a "living document." A professor elaborates, "The university's first commitment is to truth within a broadly Christian framework: Everything we do must be devoted to that." A father asserts that he sent his daughter to Christian because "I believe in the morals that the president espouses here." A

This chapter originally appeared as Tierney, W. G. (1991). Academic work and institutional culture: Constructing knowledge. *The Review of Higher Education, 14*(2), 199–216.

philosophy professor relates, "A debate on abortion happened here recently, but it was unique. We had never thought to have a debate about it before. Everyone knows that it's wrong. Even the speaker for abortion didn't believe it, but took the position as a devil's advocate."

Yet, despite the unanimity in interpreting what Christian University is, how the participants conceive of knowledge is changing. The role of a religious institution in the first years of the 21st century is no longer as clear as it once was. "I want us to be a first-class Christian university," worries a faculty member, "but I don't know what that means." "Do we evangelize in the classroom, or do we talk about business ethics and morals?" queries a business professor. According to another faculty member, "We should be working within a broadly Christian framework. 'What does it mean to be a Christian?' The standard by which we should see if we're doing okay is to see how the curriculum illuminates our understanding of our own lives." A young humanities professor adds,

> I know that the way we see things is different. But how we come together as a faculty and define what's what is anyone's guess. I could teach at the [public] university in town. They offered me a job. I stayed here because we have a better chance of defining ourselves. I'm not just a humanities professor; I'm a Christian humanities professor at an institution that claims our faith defines what we do.

Christian University is one of seven institutions I studied to investigate the curriculum in higher education from a cultural perspective. I analyzed the data from a critical framework of culture (Lather, 1986; Simon & Dippo, 1986; Tierney, 1989a, 1989b). That is, unlike some writers who have used culture as a metaphor ("an organization is *like a* culture"), I have used it as a synonym: an organization *is* a culture. As I will elaborate, a culture has an ideology that helps determine how knowledge gets defined. The work of Clifford Geertz (1973, 1983), Michel Foucault (1970, 1972, 1980), and Henry Giroux (1983, 1988) has informed my thinking. As a result of this perspective, what I say in this chapter differs from current assumptions about the production of knowledge.

I have two goals for this chapter. First, I will highlight how participants in different institutions conceive of and construct knowledge. My analysis will delineate how different constituencies in institutions use the curriculum to act out their conception of knowledge. I disagree with Burton Clark (1983) and others (Beyer & Lodahl, 1976; Lodahl & Gordon, 1972), who assert that disciplinary activity is the agent of knowledge production; I claim that institutional contexts more powerfully influence the way we define knowledge than we have previously thought.

My point is not simply to suggest that institutions cultivate the production of knowledge more intensively than do the disciplines. It is not a question of which comes first in producing knowledge—the institutional chicken or the disciplinary egg. Rather—and this is the second purpose of this chapter—knowledge is a discourse constantly reconstructed over time and place. The production of knowledge cannot be separated from the contingencies and continuous reconstruction of culture that individuals experience in their work lives. As a consequence, knowledge cannot be arbitrarily divorced from organizational ideologies.

In addition to Christian University, I will consider two other institutions, which I have named Classics College and Cutting Edge College. All three institutions are part of a larger study concerned with curricular change. To summarize that study, I made two weeklong visits to each institution during the course of an academic year and used ethnographic techniques to gather data (Spradley, 1979; Wilcox, 1980). During the investigation, I analyzed data from over 250 individuals in seven institutions. The institutions were all four-year colleges and universities located throughout the United States, both public and private, single sex and coed. (For a fuller description of the study, see Tierney, 1989b.)

Critical Ethnography

I followed a relatively new approach in qualitative research, tentatively called "critical ethnography." That is, in addition to a critical framework for the theoretical scaffolding, I used a methodology informed by critical theory. Although the basic tenets of this approach have been widely applied in anthropology, the approach is still relatively new in higher education. It heeds the anthropological call for delineating the researcher's preconceived notions of the people under study (McLaren, 1989; McLaughlin, 1992; Tierney, 1991; Willis, 1977). My purpose here is not to test hypotheses or homogenize the cacophony of voices that make up an organization, but rather to bring that polyphony to life for the reader.

First, I will briefly discuss the disciplinary conception of academic work, contrast that view with a cultural view of academic work, and use the institutional participants' comments about curriculum to outline their conceptions of knowledge. I will conclude with a discussion of the similarities and differences in how the three institutions construct knowledge and suggest three implications of a culturally constructed view of knowledge for researchers and administrators.

The Disciplinary View of Generating Knowledge

In *The Higher Education System*, Clark (1983) writes, "Despite the common tendency to overlook the importance of the disciplines, it can readily be seen as primary. . . . The discipline rather than the institution tends to become the dominant force in the working lives of academics" (p. 30). Tony Becher (1987) and Donald Light (1974), among others, agree that the disciplines define and advance knowledge. Light, for example, states, "In the world of scholarship, the activities . . . center on each discipline" (p.12).

This discipline-dependent view of knowledge assumes that knowledge consists of accumulating facts around a common intellectual discourse. A discipline's subject matter reflects natural categories that have developed over time. Some specialized fields spin off and gain academic legitimacy, as biochemistry developed from biology and chemistry. Yvonna Lincoln (1986) views such intellectual expansion of fields as "taxonomic and accretionary." She states, "We learn something and it is added to something else, and now we have two pieces of knowledge, pyramid style" (p. 139). In short, according to this view, people learn specific kinds of information within a discipline that demand the creation of a new discipline.

The implication for scholars is that they will likely have more in common with other practitioners of their individual discipline than with faculty members in other fields at their institution. As Becher (1987) observes, "If the nineteenth century still held out the promise of a common university culture, and with it perhaps a truly unified academic profession, the developments of the twentieth century progressively undermined that promise" (p. 278). Thus, the department has emerged as the basic element of the modern university; the discipline directs intellectual change, and disciplinary activity takes place, not on an institutional level, but on a departmental level. The institution has become, in Clark's (1983) words, "a holding company" (p. 34). The norms, beliefs, myths, and work of academics are determined within the discipline.

Approaching this topic from another direction, we might ask what forces outside the discipline foster knowledge production. An obvious answer is the needs of the larger society. Society's desire for a cure for AIDS, for example, has promoted knowledge generation in such fields as molecular and cellular biology. In an earlier era, the space program prompted advances in chemistry. Again, society's needs are answered by the discipline, not by the institution.

Following Clark's chain of thought, Walter Metzger (1987, p. 147) has broken these forms of disciplinary change into two branches. *Substantive growth* occurs when new subject matter is absorbed within the discipline. *Reactive growth* occurs within the discipline because of a heightened demand for professional services. In this view, society intrudes on disciplinary knowledge only when it needs a particular kind of service. And even when society comes in contact with the discipline, the scientist remains in command of the production of knowledge.

This view assumes that the accumulation of knowledge is a scientific undertaking that has to be verified by a method based on replicability and predictability. Science is free of any ideological apparatus and, in general, works outside of social forces. The scientists within a discipline have a shared idea of the underlying rationale and suppositions of their work. As George Keller (1986) states, "The world is assumed to be lawful, and the role of scientists is to discover these laws and explain how the world operates according to these laws" (p. 130). Objectivity is essential. Natural or social sciences are distinguished by their ability to meet the rigors of scientific validity. Social scientists struggle to approximate natural science's method. Thus, we use words such as "hard" and "pure" for the disciplines of chemistry and physics, and "soft" and "applied" for the less rigorous disciplines of anthropology and education.

The Cultural View of Generating Knowledge

Without disputing that the disciplines play a crucial role in organizing academic work, I take exception to the disciplinarians' generalization. I see the knowledge that disciplines produce as neither natural nor objective. Instead, what takes place within a discipline is a discourse constituted by the discipline and a variety of other social agencies. I start by assuming that the production of knowledge is socially constructed. By this I mean that participants define knowledge according to their social and historical contexts. Examples of similar lines of thinking have been developed by such feminist scholars as

Sandra Harding (1986), Karin Knorr-Cetina (1981), and Knorr-Cetina and Michael Mulkay (1983).

The point is not that knowledge advances serendipitously, but, rather, that the way disciplines define knowledge is constantly reinterpreted and redefined; social institutions and forces combine to determine what accounts for knowledge at a particular moment in history. Rather than assuming that the disciplines expand knowledge and discourse only in a taxonomic fashion, we also need to consider how disciplines limit knowledge production. As Giroux (1983) notes, "To be part of a discipline means to ask certain questions, to use a particular set of terms, and to study a relatively narrow set of things" (p. 34).

And these questions, terms, and "narrow set[s] of things" interact with institutional and faculty cultures. Knowledge is not something lying "out there," unconnected to a faculty member's experience and sense of self. Instead, the canon of what counts as knowledge concerns our assumptions about the nature of knowledge. In other words, the argument revolves around how different constituencies' discourses produce and interpret knowledge, instead of how they describe and accumulate knowledge. Giroux (1988) points out that assuming disciplines accumulate knowledge "leaves the impression that a [discipline] has a permanent character and that specific structures can be described in an essentialist manner" (p. 150). I am suggesting the opposite: disciplines are continually reconstituted and reconstructed.

Rather than assuming that knowledge is the disciplinary accumulation of a coherent frame of thinking, I consider knowledge a social product with political roots. Knowledge, then, is not simply the accumulation of objective facts that can be taught in a classroom or advanced in a laboratory. Knowledge has political consequences that shape the way we interpret and exist in the world. Of course, I cannot investigate knowledge that is decontextualized from the specific practices that surround its production. Mas'ud Zavarzadeh and Donald Morton (1987) comment that such a notion enables

> the student to see that his or her understanding of all of culture's texts
> (from philosophical treatises to popular television shows) is a result of situatedness in a complex network of gender, class and race relations and to
> see that reading (and meaning) changes depending on whether the reader

is a male or female reader, a Hispanic or white American reader, a working class reader or upper-class reader." (p. 19)

The question, then, is not how the disciplines produce knowledge, but how knowledge is conceived and used in many different contexts and situations. Of necessity, we must investigate the manifold institutions where knowledge is located and determine what the participants believe about knowledge. Seen in this light, the relationship of knowledge to ideology becomes clearer. As I use the term in this chapter, *ideology* refers to participants' assumptions about the nature of knowledge. In the words of Marilyn Schuster and Susan Van Dyne (1984), ideology is "a dynamic system of values and priorities, conscious and unconscious, by which men and women organize their actions and expectations, and explain their choices" (p. 417). As we will see, the ideology of the institution legitimates particular definitions of knowledge and discredits others.

From this perspective, culture, ideology, and knowledge are closely intertwined. Culture is the symbolic-expressive acts of human beings that occur within an organization. Within an organizational web of culture, ideology refers "to that part . . . which is actively concerned with the establishment and defense of patterns of belief and value" (Geertz, 1973, p. 231). Ideology, then, is a map of the cultural web. Knowledge is the way individuals interpret and react to the culture and ideology of the various social institutions and contexts in which they find themselves.

Thus, while the disciplinary view assumes that knowledge is a static entity, this alternative view assumes that a dynamic process helps produce and define the organizational world in which we reside. In other words, knowledge organizes a particular way of understanding the world. In this light, knowledge, ideology, and culture continuously interact with one another; a change in one will cause change in another. For example, a cultural shift in the organization brought on by a new leader may challenge both the ideology of the institution and the way the participants define knowledge.

To expand on these ideas, I turn to Classics College and Cutting Edge College. Classics College exemplifies an institution where knowledge is seemingly generated by the discipline, and Cutting Edge College is an institution where the participants have eschewed the discipline in favor of the institution. Once I have sketched portraits of the two colleges, I will consider the nature of knowledge and its relationship to institutional and faculty cultures at Classics, Cutting Edge, and Christian University.

Classics College

Although competition to get into 80-year-old Classics College is not terrifically intense, the student body is considered one of the most intelligent in the country. Student enrollment is slightly over 1,000, and full-time faculty number around 100. Classics College has a long history of teaching "the classics." Many faculty members feel that the institution's purpose is constant and clear. "We believe we are an educational institution," observes one longtime faculty, "and not a social hostel, or a training program to get along with people, or a 'how to' vocational school. We are dedicated to education." By *education*, the professor means that students must have a firm understanding and knowledge of Western civilization. A faculty member for many years at Classics says, "We teach people how to think. We haven't gone in for fads. We've stayed right because we *are* right."

A student comments on the curriculum: "They really make you think. I've learned so much about my past, about Western culture and society. It's intense. Sometimes I think it's too bad we don't learn about other cultures, but you can't learn everything. I feel I'm getting a well-rounded education."

The institutional culture of Classics ostensibly reflects the disciplines; consequently, the organizational structure centers around traditionally defined departments. Departments are filled with scholars with doctorates in areas such as English literature or biology. The school features virtually no interdisciplinary departments such as women's studies or African American studies. Over the years, faculty and administrators have, indeed, discussed the merits of including "nontraditional" curricula but have always decided against "fads."

However, the downside of these attributes also emerges from the interviews. The president warns, "Departments are too strong. People's interests lie in the departments, in their specialty areas." A faculty member comments, "The place has been governed by a powerful educational ideology that is tied to change in the fields." The speaker's comment pertains to how traditional disciplines have increased the information one needs to know, while the epistemological underpinnings of the discipline have remained the same. A third person concurs: "I'm constantly reading in my area. I can't imagine trying to work across disciplines when there is so much happening in my own discipline." The picture arises, then, of an institution where the faculty culture mirrors the disciplinary culture. A faculty member who recently arrived from teaching at another institution shakes her head over the "very old-fashioned notions" she found at Classics. "Greeks and Romans and Christians! I'm amazed there's such a slow process" of curricular change. She adds ironically, "I'm still astonished that the Symposium isn't taught. We are intellectually out of date. And we talk about interdisciplinary work, but it's a joke when I think about other places I've been."

Interdisciplinary coursework at Classics means that faculty from different disciplines lecture in the humanities core required of all students. "There's no synthesis going on," says a humanities professor. "There's no dialogue across the disciplines. One individual comes into class and does his thing, and then the next week another person comes in and does his thing." At Classics, most innovation occurs within the major; little college-wide reform takes place. A senior faculty member agrees, "We are extremely conservative. We were innovative fifty years ago and haven't been ever since."

Given the faculty's disdain for "fads," many of the recent critics of higher education will find much to like at Classics. Allan Bloom (1987), for example, comments, "I have heard the abandonment of requirements to learn languages or philosophy or science lauded as a progress of openness. . . . To be open to knowing, there are certain kinds of things one must know" (p. 41). This approach assumes that there is a unity to knowledge and that one purpose of the curriculum is to provide the essential building blocks of knowledge so that people are free to think.

"That idea is absurd," states a dissident professor at Classics when I summarize Bloom's argument. Bloom and his followers are "against 'isms' which usually means feminism." In the words of Schuster and Van Dyne (1984), what is occurring at Classics is that faculty members work from an "invisible paradigm" where knowledge is removed from its context. "Inevitably," they note, "invisible paradigms are related to ideology. The more coherent an ideology and the better it serves the interests of those who benefit from the status quo, the less visible these paradigms will be to those who perpetuate them" (p. 417). From this perspective, the lives of women, people of color, and sexual minorities are marginalized and trivialized.

The invisible paradigm, then, exists as the sum of curricular offerings that serve as knowledge. "Everything remains the same," comments one professor at Classics. "We provide the same framework, the same values and practices. The canon of what we know as knowledge may have been revised to include a new author, but the assumptions about the nature of knowledge remain the same." In other words, at Classics College, to be knowledgeable in 1990 means essentially what it did 50 years ago except for the inclusion of a few different authors on reading lists.

In such a system, the discipline guides the change of institutional knowledge. A biochemistry professor explains: "The nature of my discipline—the knowledge in it—is being developed so fast. We don't do interdisciplinary things here because just to keep up in my discipline is next to impossible." Although biochemistry may look like a hybrid to many, this professor speaks quite clearly about what guides his thinking and what kind of knowledge needs to inform the curriculum. Faculty members identify with their discipline, which in turn defines what will be taught. The assumption follows Bloom's (1987) line of thinking; students need to be socialized—"there are certain things one must know"—and the discipline defines what those "things" are.

Cutting Edge College

Full-time student enrollment at Cutting Edge College is a little over 1000; faculty size hovers around 90. The student body is bright and articulate and is drawn from throughout the country. Cutting Edge, barely a quarter-century old, has a well-earned reputation for being left of center, politically and intellectually. The campus sits in an idyllic, semi-rural setting.

Various faculty members speak about the purpose of their curriculum in terms that are antithetical to the notion of knowledge as facts and figures. "We believe that in general disciplinary knowledge is the product of a historical accident," comments one person. "We need to explode the myth that someone can master a concrete entity called 'knowledge,'" adds another. A student comments, "I'm made to question where I fit in the grand scheme of things. I constantly am brought back to myself, to my relationship to what we're learning. What this place teaches you is how to get your hands on the knowledge, to access knowledge."

Interdisciplinary work is essential, and departmental boundaries are absent. Instead, the faculty work in schools that are interdisciplinary and act as cross-fertilizers for one another. At Cutting Edge, it is more common to see an individual trained in English literature co-teaching with someone in economics or biology than to see three English faculty teaching a course. One individual comments:

> The curriculum is fragmented, purposefully so. People need to cut it up into different pieces, take knowledge apart and put it back together again. We want students to make the synthesis and connections for themselves. Somewhere after World War II it became impossible to think of all knowledge existing in one paradigm. We're in a different world now, and we want to enable our students to grasp onto the power structures.

As with Christian University and Classics College, the culture of Cutting Edge has contributed to what the participants view as legitimate knowledge. "It's important for us to be [on the] cutting edge," says an administrator, pointing out a key precept. Institutional culture highlights particular pieces of knowledge that the participants seek to legitimate and, just as important, subsumes other knowledge forms that remain hidden or discredited.

One individual explains, "I put together a course, and then one or two of my colleagues go over it. They really make me rethink it, too! Sometimes I will drop in on someone's course just to pick up something people are doing that I don't know about." It is interesting to note that these courses he sits in on are not in his discipline. Another faculty member comments: "The ability to converse with people, to drop in on one another, is what makes Cutting Edge special." Another person confirms the interdisciplinary nature of the institution: "The institution gives you the freedom and space and helps to make connections across boundaries. Your concerns and interests affect you on a curricular level."

At Cutting Edge, the culture of the institution has become more prominent than the culture of the discipline. The following discussion about how curriculum is shaped at Cutting Edge highlights the difference between it and Classics:

Faculty #1: The disciplines give us no clues, no help whatsoever.
Faculty #2: If I published in my field, in the *American Political Science Review*, people around here would say, "That's too bad!"
Faculty #3: I don't know what it would be like if we couldn't work with one another. The reward is in the ability to work with other faculty.

Faculty #4: There's a collegiality that's forced on you. Sure, we fight and yell, just like a family. But I'm stunned at how many people are alienated elsewhere.

Faculty #3: The collegiality is just great. I went to a women's studies dinner the other night. I wouldn't do that if I were at another place.

Faculty #1: You need an intellectual center of gravity to create a curriculum, and people have relied on the disciplines for that, but the disciplines are dead.

Faculty #2: To some extent, we create our own cutting edge.

Faculty #4: I hope in the future we work out a few more coherent courses of study. Feminist studies, law . . .

Faculty #3: Cultural studies.

Faculty #4: More on the third world, gender.

Faculty #1: But the faculty will continue to drive the change. Encouragement can come from the administration, but not the decisions. What's good is that they encourage, foster change.

This discussion is typical of conversations that take place frequently at Cutting Edge. Of interest here is the faculty's pride in what they perceive as the institution's uniqueness. Perhaps these perceptions are somewhat exaggerated. For example, it is conceivable that speaker #3 would go to a women's studies dinner at another institution, even though she says she would not. Speaker #4 has found alienated faculty elsewhere, but certainly not all faculty at other institutions are alienated. Equally certain, other faculties can have radically different views of knowledge—Christian University comes to mind. And surely speaker #1's comment about the administration fostering change could be said at many other campuses. Yet the culture of Cutting Edge clearly provides its faculty with an identity that lets them define the perimeters of knowledge, and, as a result, they know who they are in relation to that knowledge.

As with the other two institutions, Cutting Edge has negative aspects to its approach. A new faculty member comments that the common term for this curricular approach to knowledge is " 'mode of inquiry' because we don't lecture, we want discussion. In general I like it, but I worry sometimes that they're missing something. I think my students should know about the Licensing Act of 1737, but how do I get that across?"

Her concern echoes that of the biochemistry professor at Classics: "What do students need to know?" The difference in curricular formulae between Classics and Cutting Edge is that Classics assumes that all well-educated people must know certain data, whereas Cutting Edge denies the assumption that knowledge is ever neutral and, hence, that "to be educated" means one knows a particular body of knowledge. Furthermore, Classics College assumes that students will never be able to think independently until they master particular information; being educated is being able to think. Conversely, Cutting Edge College assumes that mastering knowledge is a subjective undertaking that must be understood as political. Although critical inquiry is the subject of learning at both institutions, Classics faculty work from one particular ideology, and Cutting Edge's faculty work from another. Knowledge is legitimized by the discipline in the former, and by the institution in the latter.

Discussion

I have portrayed Classics College, Cutting Edge College, and Christian University to highlight two points. First, individuals in institutions have unique ways of defining knowledge; as a result, such definitions differ from institution to institution. Thus, the disciplines are not solely responsible for encouraging knowledge production. Institutional contexts have a more powerful influence on how we define knowledge than we have previously thought. Think about similarities and differences in the ways the individuals at the three institutions construct their versions of what counts for knowledge.

At Classics, the institution's participants encourage students to objectify knowledge and see if they can make sense of it. The knowledge explosion within each discipline has led to much emphasis on disciplinary rigor. Students are not taught to see themselves as part of the process they study. Linking knowledge to a student's life is not considered important.

At Cutting Edge College, people acknowledge that students can graduate from the institution without having come into contact with certain disciplines or certain facts. A professor states, "Does it bother me that a student can graduate without enough coursework in the sciences, or that a kid might not have dabbled enough in the quantitative area? To be honest with you, yeah, it bothers me. Should we do anything about it, such as change requirements? Absolutely not." Other faculty at Cutting Edge concur. Comments one: "We have a philosophical stance about knowledge. It's explicit, clear."

Cutting Edge College tries to make students see how what is being taught affects their lives.

The participants at Christian University used to have an extremely clear conception of knowledge based on the basic tenets of their faith. Although the clarity has blurred a bit, the institution still has the clearest view of knowledge of the three. More than Classics or Cutting Edge, participants at Christian University have concerned themselves with socializing students toward a particular worldview. Knowledge is linked to and determined by the underpinnings of the participants' faith. Their understanding of what counts for knowledge is determined by an ideological process through which the various participants experience themselves, their relation to others, and the institution's relationship to society. Recall the student, for example, who commented that he attended the institution because the basic teachings of the university—the institutional definition of knowledge—reinforced his beliefs.

We see, then, the inherent differences in the way the institutions come to grips with and, ultimately, define knowledge. The faculty member at Christian University sees himself as a *Christian* humanities professor. The religious life of the institution labels some courses and knowledge as taboo. The biology department does not routinely discuss abortion or, for that matter, evolution. At Classics College, a faculty member defines knowledge from within the confines of the discipline. The culture of the institution overlays a view of knowledge as if knowledge were defined by the discipline. At Cutting Edge College, the faculty eschew disciplines, epitomized by the faculty member who would disdain publishing in his field's major journal and the faculty member who talked about how knowledge needs to be constantly "cut up" and put together in different forms and shapes.

I also found similarities among the institutions. Classics and Cutting Edge do not equate vocational skills with knowledge. Students only coincidentally receive information that prepares them for the world of work. Instead of specific technical knowledge, the institutions provide them with an introduction to understanding how systems operate. Interestingly, Cutting Edge College and Christian University are also alike in their tolerance for faculty diversity. "A conservative, macho economist wouldn't make it here," comments a longtime faculty member at Cutting Edge—presumably not because this hypothetical individual is either an economist or a male but because the culture of the institution would frown on both "conservative" and "macho" people. Similarly, Christian University would not hire a radical feminist or an existential philosopher. The "conservative, macho" economist or the radical feminist have conceptions of knowledge that are at odds with the ideology of the institutions.

As these case studies show, institutions in some way play a role in interpreting knowledge. Now we turn to the second point of this chapter. Knowledge is a social construct undergoing interpretation and change on a variety of levels and in a variety of social contexts. As organizational participants construct their reality, they also construct what counts for knowledge. Thus, rather than being neutral and taxonomic, knowledge is produced and legitimized by the ideological and cultural processes at work in the organization.

My point goes further than the observation that different institutions have different definitions of knowledge. I am suggesting that knowledge is produced through the construction of forms of culture and ideology that need to be analyzed for their wider social and political significance. By attempting to come to terms with how institutional participants define knowledge, we raise questions about the historical and material conditions in which we find ourselves. In doing so, we are forced to consider whose interests are served by how we define knowledge and whose are silenced.

Conclusion

By pointing out the fragmentation that exists about what counts as knowledge, I run the risk of painting a relativistic portrait of institutions and knowledge. As Geertz (1983) observes: "The view that thought is where you find it, that you find it in all sorts of cultural shapes and social sizes . . . is somehow taken to be a claim that there is nothing to say except when in Rome, to each his own. . . . But there is a great deal more to say" (p. 154).

I agree. I offer three suggestions about ideology, faculty culture, and institutional culture drawn from my analysis. They are academic areas that warrant further consideration by researchers and administrators, not a blueprint for administrative action.

Ideology

I argue that we should not tie ideology to particular interest groups but think of it instead as part of a cultural system (Tierney, 1991). The ideological apparatus of the institution seems to play a more determined role than previously thought. At one time, we believed that only those institutions with sagas (Clark, 1970, 1972) provided guidelines by which participants could find meaning and identity. I think that institutional ideology goes much further; even in institutions without a clearly delineated saga, the strength of what its perceived mission statement says or does not say helps define the perimeters for action and discourse and virtually dictates how knowledge is defined.

Faculty Culture

The cultures of the faculty and the tensions experienced between the faculty cultures and institutional culture also demand further analysis and reformulation. As Giroux (1988) notes, "The intellectual is more than a person of letters, or a producer and transmitter of ideas. Intellectuals are also mediators, legitimators, and producers of ideas and social practices; they perform a function eminently political in nature" (p. 151). That is, the nature of relationships that take place within an institution both comes from and transforms the participants' view of knowledge. If faculty exist in different cultures, then we need to understand more fully the contradictions among the various cultures if, for example, we are to orchestrate curricular change in a more coherent fashion.

Institutional Culture

Pedagogical practices, teacher-student interactions, faculty-faculty interactions, and a host of other cultural variables come into play because of the participants' definition of knowledge. Think of Cutting Edge College, where a cultural standard is that faculty work with one another across disciplines, in contrast to Classics College, where the psychology department is not on speaking terms with the natural science division because natural scientists believe the knowledge in the discipline of psychology is beneath them. Recall the parent and student at Christian University who view teaching and learning as a means of receiving the established truths that the faculty possess.

We thus begin to see how the discourses produced about knowledge locate specific social practices and relations and how such discussions ultimately link up to become a relationship between ideology and culture. To come to terms with the relationship of culture, ideology, and knowledge, we need to investigate microscopic aspects of institutional life to gain a fuller version of the constructed realities of the participants.

References

Becher, T. (1987). The disciplinary shaping of the profession. In B. Clark (Ed.), *The academic profession: National, disciplinary, and institutional settings* (pp. 271–303). Berkeley: University of California Press.

Beyer, J., & Lodahl, T. M. (1976). A comparative study of patterns of influence in United States and English universities. *Administrative Science Quarterly, 21,* 104–129.

Bloom, A. (1987). *The closing of the American mind.* New York: Simon and Schuster.

Clark, B. (1970). *The distinctive college.* Chicago, IL: Aldine.

Clark, B. (1972). The organizational saga in higher education. *Administrative Science Quarterly, 17*(2), 178–184.

Clark, B. (1983). *The higher education system: Academic organization in cross-national perspective.* Berkeley: University of California Press.

Foucault, M. (1970). *The order of things.* New York: Pantheon.

Foucault, M. (1972). *The archaeology of knowledge.* New York: Pantheon.

Foucault, M. (1980). *Power/knowledge.* New York: Pantheon.

Geertz, C. (1973). *The interpretation of cultures.* New York: Basic Books.

Geertz, C. (1983). *Local knowledge.* New York: Basic Books.

Giroux, H. A. (1983). *Theory and resistance in education: A pedagogy for the opposition.* South Hadley, MA: Bergin & Garvey.

Giroux, H. A. (1988). *Teachers as intellectuals.* Granby, MA: Bergin & Garvey.

Harding, S. (1986). *The science question in feminism.* Ithaca, NY: Cornell University Press.

Keller, G. (1986). Free at last? Breaking the chains that bind education research. *The Review of Higher Education, 10*(2), 129–134.

Knorr-Cetina, K. (1981). *The manufacture of knowledge.* Oxford, UK: Pergamon.

Knorr-Cetina, K., & Mulkay, M. (Eds.). (1983). *Science observed: Perspectives on the social study of science.* Beverly Hills, CA: Sage.

Lather, P. (1986). Issues of validity in openly ideological research: Between a rock and a soft place. *Interchange, 17*(4), 63–84.

Light, D., Jr. (1974). The structure of the academic professions. *Sociology of Education, 47,* 2–28.

Lincoln, Y. (1986). A future-oriented comment on the state of the profession. *The Review of Higher Education, 10*(2), 135–142.

Lodahl, J., & Gordon, G. (1972). The structure of scientific fields and the functioning of university graduate departments. *American Sociological Review, 37,* 57–72.

McLaren, P. (1989). *Life in schools.* New York: Longman.

McLaughlin, D. (1992). *When literacy empowers: Navajo language in print.* Albuquerque, NM: University of New Mexico Press.

Metzger, W. (1987). The academic profession in the United States. In B. Clark (Ed.), *The academic profession: National, disciplinary, and institutional settings* (pp. 123–208). Berkeley: University of California Press.

Schuster, M., & Van Dyne, S. (1984). Placing women in the liberal arts: Stages of curriculum transformation. *Harvard Educational Review, 54*(4), 413–428.

Simon, R., & Dippo, D. (1986). On critical ethnographic work. *Anthropology and Education Quarterly, 17*(34), 195–202.

Spradley, J. (1979). *The ethnographic interview.* New York: Holt.

Tierney, W. G. (1989a). Cultural politics and the curriculum in postsecondary education. *Boston University Journal of Education, 171*(3), 72–88.

Tierney, W. G. (1989b). *Curricular landscapes, democratic vistas: Transformative leadership in higher education.* New York: Praeger.

Tierney, W. G. (1991). *Culture and ideology in higher education: Advancing a critical agenda.* New York: Praeger.

Wilcox, K. (1980). *The ethnography of schooling: Implications for educational policy making.* Project Report No. 80-a-10. Washington, DC: National Institute of Education.

Willis, P. (1977). *Learning to labor: How working class kids get working class jobs.* New York: Columbia University Press.

Zavarzadeh, M., & Morton, D. (1987). War of the words: The battle of (and for) English. *In These Times, 12,* 18–19.

5

AN ANTHROPOLOGICAL
ANALYSIS OF STUDENT
PARTICIPATION IN COLLEGE

The fundamental factor that keeps Indians and
non-Indians from communicating is that they are
speaking about two entirely different perceptions of the world.

—Vine Deloria Jr., *The Metaphysics
of Modern Existence*

In this chapter I take issue with Tinto's widely accepted theoretical
model that views college participation as if it were a "rite of passage,"
where academic and social integration is essential for student persistence. First, I argue that Tinto has misinterpreted the anthropological notions of ritual, and in doing so, he has created a theoretical construct with
practical implications that hold potentially harmful consequences for racial
and ethnic minorities. I critique the epistemological argument Tinto has articulated—that of social integration—from a cultural perspective informed
by critical theory (Fay, 1987; Foster, 1989; Giroux, 1988, 1990; Tierney, 1993).
That is, I take a social constructionist view of reality, and I operate from the
perspective that the purpose of our theoretical models is not merely to describe the world, but to change it.

I then highlight the practical or "real world" implications of a social
integrationist stance by deconstructing the discourse of two college administrators who were part of a two-year investigation pertaining to the college-
going patterns of American Indian college students (Tierney, 1992). The administrators describe how they perceived Native American students' attendance at their institutions. The assumption here is that the ideas and

This chapter originally appeared as Tierney, W. G. (1992). An anthropological analysis of student participation in college. *The Journal of Higher Education, 63*(6), 603–618.

discourse that speakers utilize influence the actions that occur on their campuses. And in large part, those actions and policies have been ineffectual in stemming the tide of minority student departure in general and Native American leave-taking in particular. I conclude by suggesting that rather than think about student participation from a social integrationist perspective, an alternative model is to conceive of universities as multicultural entities where difference is highlighted and celebrated. Accordingly, if we want our colleges and universities to be multicultural, we need theoretical models different from those of the social integrationists, which in turn will call for different assumptions about reality and what must be done to engage college students.

A caveat is in order. This is an essay in the root sense of the word—a trial of some ideas. By taking issue with a theorist's notions or deconstructing the words of an individual, one runs the risk of painting heroes and villains, of encasing one theory as morally wrong and another as politically correct. The argument here, however, is neither to canonize one discourse over another nor to accentuate the foibles of any administrator. Rather, the chapter seeks to provoke dialogue by taking issue with some of the most commonly held perceptions we currently have about college life, about students, and about how we think about cultural difference and the need to develop more culturally responsive ways to engage minority students.

Perspectives on College Participation: Theory

Tinto's Model and Rituals of Integration

Over the past several decades, a variety of researchers have sought to understand why some students leave college and others remain (Astin, 1977; Bean & Metzner, 1985; Spady, 1970). Indeed, one could argue that student departure has been the central focus of higher education research. In general, much of this research has tried to delineate different causal variables that might plausibly lead to the retention of students. The search for an understanding about why students leave college is not merely of theoretical interest; if a model may be built that explains student departure, then it may be possible for colleges to retain students. The successful retention of students offers at least three benefits: the student will be able to reap the rewards that a college degree affords, the college or university will be able to maintain the income that derives from the student's attendance, and society will be able to utilize the skills of students in becoming more productive. Clearly, it is to everyone's benefit to come to terms with why students leave college.

Such a concern is particularly germane in a discussion about minority student achievement. Researchers have long documented the underrepresentation of racial and ethnic minorities in academe. For the purpose of this chapter, we may add that American Indian involvement in postsecondary institutions is of particular concern. Although researchers differ about the precise percentages of Native Americans who attend college, everyone is in agreement about gross averages, and those averages highlight problems throughout the academic pipeline. If 100 students are in ninth grade, about 60 of them will graduate from high school, and about 20 will enter academe. Of those 20 students, only about 3 will eventually receive a four-year degree (Tierney, 1992).

Researchers have been able to discover that certain characteristics in a student's background help or hinder one's persistence in college. For example, we have learned that if a student's parents have gone to college, the student is more likely to attend and to graduate from college than is a student whose parents did not go to a postsecondary institution. We know that an individual whose brothers or sisters have attended college is more likely to persist in college than the young man or woman whose siblings have not participated in college. We know that someone who has had an academic track in high school is more likely to attend a four-year college than is someone who has pursued a vocational track.

We also have learned a great deal about gross characteristics that pertain to race and class. As noted, an individual who is White is more likely to go to college than is someone who is African American or Native American. Someone whose parents earn over $80,000 a year is more likely to attend a four-year institution than is someone whose parents are on welfare. Although each of these pieces of information may have helped researchers in predicting the success of students, such individualistic characteristics have stymied researchers in their search for a general causal model of student participation. In turn, minority student participation in academe has remained problematic.

Vincent Tinto (1975, 1982, 1987) has developed a theoretical model that takes into account the individualistic pieces of information such as those just reported, but he has done so in a manner that is comprehensive rather than particularistic. That is, Tinto has sought to explain why students leave college by calling upon a framework that incorporates factors such as family income or student background. He has used such information not as an end in itself but to develop a general theory of student participation as opposed to an individualistic analysis of why one or another student is likely to attend and eventually graduate.

In doing so, Tinto has worked in the tradition of other researchers, such as Spady (1970, 1971), by asking two central questions: (1) what are those bonding mechanisms that integrate students into the life of the institution, and (2) how might postsecondary institutions and students be theoretically conceived? A significant number of researchers have accepted Tinto's basic formula and have returned to testing specific variables to see whether the model holds up under scrutiny when different characteristics are analyzed. As Stage (1990) has noted, "Today few would question that students' commitment, academic integration, and social integration are crucial to their academic success" (p. 250).

Following Spady, Tinto developed his model by calling upon the work of two prominent social theorists of the early 20th century—Emile Durkheim and Arnold Van Gennep. Durkheim, considered by many to be the father of modern sociology, posited that the degree to which an individual was integrated into the fabric of societal institutions lessened the likelihood that someone experienced anomie. In turn, the less one experienced anomie, the less likely that individual was to commit suicide. Thus, by manipulating a variety of characteristics drawn from data about European countries, Durkheim (1951) showed how married Italian Catholics in tightly knit families in small towns, for example, were less likely to commit suicide than were unmarried urban Protestant Englishmen.

Van Gennep (1960) was an anthropologist who studied tribal societies; in particular he investigated "rites de passage." Rites of passage in a particular culture were rituals designed to move individuals from one developmental stage to another. These rituals took place throughout an individual's life. The most obvious rites of passage in tribal societies occurred for young men and women when they were to assume the mantle of adulthood. Although the actual rituals differed dramatically from culture to culture in both act and duration, Van Gennep argued that all cultures had rituals that functioned in similar fashion. In effect, as a functionalist, Van Gennep believed that rituals were a crucial mechanism necessary to every tribal society. Without such rituals, the developmental patterns necessary for society's maintenance would be destroyed and the culture would not survive.

Tinto has suggested that we ought to think of colleges in light of Durkheim's and Van Gennep's work. Following Durkheim, Tinto argues that, to the degree participants are integrated into the institution's fabric, the greater likelihood exists that the individual will not develop a sense of anomie and will not commit "suicide" by leaving the institution. In effect, a college is an institution designed as a rite of passage that functions in much the same manner as ritualized institutions in other societies. Postsecondary institutions serve as functional vehicles for incorporating the young into society by way of their integration into the college or university.

Tinto is the first to acknowledge that his model is not perfect. Adult students, for example, may not necessarily fit the schema he has outlined. Tinto also has been most vocal about redirecting how researchers think of college departure, so that we no longer conceive of student leave-taking by using a pejorative term such as "dropping out" because the student may well return at another time. Nevertheless, Tinto's model also holds up well when one thinks of different populations. Traditional-age students are more likely to graduate than nontraditional-age populations. A residential institution that has an active social life is more likely to have a higher retention rate than are urban commuter institutions. Full-time students have a greater likelihood of graduating from a four-year institution than do part-time students. On one level each of these facts gives credence to Tinto's formula: to what extent institutions function as societal rites of passage, and to what degree individuals are bonded and integrated into the life of the institution, determines how likely it is that students will persist and graduate.

Most work has been in a similar vein; as noted, researchers have used different variables to test whether Tinto's model holds (Cabrera, Stampen, & Hansen, 1990; Nora, Attinasi, & Matonak, 1990). Unfortunately, those individuals who have undertaken such studies have agreed implicitly with the epistemological foundations from which Tinto has worked. To his considerable credit, Tinto has developed a conceptual model that calls for investigation and analysis at the foundational level rather than simply at the causal level. Instead of merely accepting the scaffolding upon which Tinto has built his theory, researchers need to interrogate the assumptions of that scaffolding. I turn now to one such possible interpretation and interrogation. A discussion of the foundations of social integration will highlight some essential dilemmas when considered from an anthropological perspective.

An Anthropological Analysis of Tinto's Model

As I discuss Tinto's model, it is helpful to keep in mind racial and ethnic minorities such as American Indians who attend mainstream institutions. Social integrationists assert that all individuals—regardless of race, class, or gender—must undergo a "rite of passage" to achieve full development in society. The assumption is that a uniform set of values and attitudes remains in an institution, and that it is the individual's task to adapt to the system. The problems with such a view, however, are fourfold. Two problems pertain to a misinterpretation of the cultural definition of ritual, and two problems concern an overreliance on an integrative framework.

Culture and Rituals

Consider the differences between Van Gennep's and Tinto's use of the term *ritual*. When Van Gennep wrote about rites of passage, he spoke of rituals within a specific culture. The Maori of New Zealand or the Arunta of Australia had rituals that initiated the young into society. The Ndembu of Africa had puberty rites for girls and rituals of manhood for boys (Turner, 1977). The same point, however, cannot be made of Tinto's rituals, which occur in American colleges and universities. An American Indian who sets foot on a mainstream campus undergoes a disruptive cultural experience, not because college is a rite of passage, but because the institution is culturally distinct from the Indian youth's own culture. When Van Gennep (1960) developed his functionalist theory, he never anticipated that it would be used to explain one culture's ritual to initiate a member of another culture.

The first problem with social integrationist theory, then, is that it borrows an anthropological term—ritual—yet extracts the term from its cultural foundations. One cannot speak of ritual without first considering the cultural contexts in which that ritual is embedded. In the case of American higher education, we find that colleges and universities reflect the culture of the dominant society. In America, that dominant culture is White.

To be sure, organizations such as traditionally Black institutions or tribally controlled colleges exist in the United States, but these institutions also incorporate the dominant mores of American society simply by having to meet accreditation requirements, employing faculty who come from mainstream institutions and the like (Tierney, 1992). Institutions such as tribal colleges are under perhaps the greatest pressure to conform, given the serious financial constraints in which they must operate; these institutions garner most of their income from a federal law that stipulates that they meet specified standards (Olivas, 1982, 1983). To assume that colleges and universities do not reflect the culture of mainstream society is to overlook the crucial importance of the sociocultural contexts surrounding postsecondary organizations. Simply stated, higher education's institutions have histories and current contexts that help determine their ideology and culture. Until very recently in American higher education, colleges and universities were designed to educate a clientele that was overwhelmingly composed of White males who came from the middle and upper classes.

Although critics may certainly argue with a cultural analysis of postsecondary institutions, one is hard-pressed to do so while simultaneously using as a central concept the cultural idea of a rite of passage. In short, if social integrationists are to employ an anthropological term, such as a ritual, then they must take into account the cultures in which those rituals exist. If one does so with regard to Tinto's model, one finds that he has developed an analytic tool that is dysfunctional: individuals from one culture, such as Apache, are to undergo a ritual in another culture, such as Anglo.

A second conceptual problem with the use of a ritual in academe pertains to the assumption of one's leave-taking from such a ritual. In traditional cultures rites of passage do not have notions such as "departure," "failure," or "dropout." Choice does not exist about whether to undergo the ritual; one simply does. As noted, Tinto (1982) has accurately pointed out that the use of a term such as "dropout" has negative connotations, and he has argued that one should use the term "departure" instead because it is value neutral. He has assumed, however, that departure is normal. "It seems unlikely that we will be able to greatly reduce dropouts," he has noted (1982, p. 695). Along a similar line, he added,

> There is much to be said for a system of education that serves to distinguish between those with the competence or interest, motivation, and drive to finish given courses of study, and those who, for a variety of reasons do not or simply will not seek to complete their programs. (1982, p. 695)

Although a term such as "departure" may well appear to be value neutral to those who use the term, what social integrationists overlook is that concepts such as "departure," "dropout," or "failure" are all cultural constructs. Tinto assumes that for one reason or another some students will choose not to participate in a rite of passage and other students will not complete the ritual. Yet when one considers rituals in traditional cultures, we find that an initiate chooses neither to participate nor to leave the ritual. Anthropologists George and Louise Spindler (1989) are helpful in explaining how the Arunta of Australia conceive of initiation rituals:

> Despite the onerous nature of the initiation, . . . all of the young initiates survive the ordeal and are dedicated to seeing that the next class of initiates gets the same treatment. All of the initiates succeed, none fail. . . . To fail would mean at least that one could not be an Arunta, and usually this must mean death as well, but not death at the hands of another, but social death. . . . The whole operation of the initiation school is managed to produce success. To fail to initiate the young successfully is unthinkable. The continuity of culture would be broken and the society would disintegrate. There are no dropouts. (p. 10)

Nor are there "departers." To be sure, someone may die in a "rite of passage," but the essential point here is that in traditional societies individuals do not have the option to leave their group as students do who attend a college or university. What Tinto again has failed to do is to investigate the cultural context of the anthropological term "ritual" and, in turn, to show how the language of student participation is a cultural construction. He has assumed that student departure is a universal concept rather than a cultural category developed by the society that uses the ritual. Dropouts exist in modern American schools and colleges; the term is absent from Arunta vocabulary as well as from any number of other tribal societies. The language used to think and talk about students is a cultural construct. Failure exists in postsecondary institutions before students are admitted, enrolled, or take classes. Failure or leave-taking or departure do not come in the door when students enter. Human discourse and action are cultural categories; to come to terms with these categories one must investigate the categories themselves rather than assume that actions such as leaving college are natural and universal.

Individuals and Integration

The third and fourth anthropological problems with Tinto's model pertain to the Durkheimian reliance on individuals and integration. Tinto has conceptualized college going at the individualist level rather than at a collective one. From a social integrationist perspective, individuals attend college, become integrated or not, graduate or depart. Conformity is the norm and is the responsibility of the individual. Absent from this analysis is any discussion about the cultural formations of groups. Social integrationists assume that culture exists at a meta level—all cultures are similar and the institution merely reflects the culture of society. Indeed, Tinto's book *Leaving College* (1987) emphasizes the "roots of individual departure" and a "theory of individual departure." From an anthropological standpoint, to emphasize "individual" at the expense of the "group" or the "culture" is backward. Indeed, Native American authors such as Badwound (1990), Benally (1988), McNeley (1988), Padilla and Pavel (1989), and Wright and Tierney* (1991) have effectively argued that the importance of tribal culture is crucial when thinking about the roots of student departure. Olneck (1990) has argued how critical this issue is with regard to minorities in general: "[We] must recognize . . . the identities and claims of groups *as groups* and must facilitate, or at least symbolically represent and legitimate collective identity" (p. 148, emphasis original). Again, what is particularly odd with regard to Tinto's analysis is that he uses anthropological terms in an individualist manner.

Furthermore, Tinto never takes into account, or at least never explains to readers, that he is a "native" studying "native rituals." As a faculty member at a mainstream university, he describes processes in which he partakes. The point is not that a native observer's analysis is useless. To the contrary, native perceptions of the world are essential to understanding that world, but one must necessarily accept that those understandings are provisional, subjective, and never complete. As Edmund Leach (1968) has observed, "to understand the word ritual we must take note of the user's background and prejudices" (p. 521). Indeed, in our field of study, Attinasi (1989) similarly has commented, "What are needed are naturalistic, descriptive studies guided by research perspectives that emphasize the insider's point of view" (p. 250).

---

*Not Native American.

The need to understand the user's "background and prejudices" reflects the anthropological belief that reality is socially constructed. Individuals and groups do not perceive reality in the same fashion. The researcher must come to terms not only with his or her own preconceived notions of reality and the phenomenon under study but also with those of the individuals who partake in the ritual. Yet Tinto works from a positivist framework where law-like generalizations are possible and the implicit assumptions and beliefs of both the researcher and the researched are irrelevant. Again, one may reject a cultural model that assumes reality is socially constructed, but that cannot be done while one simultaneously employs analytical tools that derive from those same cultural models.

Thus, an anthropological analysis of Tinto's model has two overarching concerns. On the one hand, rituals of transition have never been conceptualized as movements from one culture to another. Van Gennep never assumed that a Sioux youth underwent an initiation ritual in Navajo society. Yet Tinto's model assumes that same Sioux youth will undergo a rite of passage in Anglo society. On the other hand, a model of integration that never questions who is to be integrated and how it is to be done assumes an individualist stance of human nature and rejects differences based on categories such as class, race, and gender.

Such concerns bring into question Tinto's overall model; however, this discourse of integration is of particular importance when we consider college participation of underrepresented racial and ethnic groups. As Olneck (1990) has observed, the language of integration is "the voice of white middle-class education professionals speaking about 'problem' groups and about the solutions to the problems posed by diversity" (p. 163). Although Tinto and other like-minded researchers should be applauded for their attempt to shift the burden of blame for dropouts away from the victims, models of integration essentially have the effect of merely inserting minorities into a dominant cultural frame of reference that is transmitted within dominant cultural forms, leaving invisible cultural hierarchies intact (Colon, 1991).

I now turn to an example of how such implicit assumptions are played out at mainstream universities. The data derive from a two-year investigation of Native Americans on college campuses (Tierney, 1992). I undertook case studies at 10 campuses and conducted slightly over 200 interviews. The point of the following section is to analyze the discourse of two individuals to underscore how social integrationist notions get enacted.

Perspectives on College Participation: Practice

Defining the Problem

At one university, the president commented on the problems Native Americans have in college by pointing out, "They have a terrible problem with acculturation. They grow up without competition, and when they come here to a university whose ethic is achievement and competition, it's tough." At a second institution, a top administrator added, "The major problem is that they have a foot in each culture that draws them back to their roots. They are drawn back to their own culture and it's a difficult transition to make. It's a real problem that's not easy for us to solve."

I offer these comments for two reasons. First, they are commonplace. I consistently heard similar kinds of observations from other individuals. Second, these comments logically accompany the social integrationist position. Following the recent deconstructionist work of Rhoades (1990), Rhoades and Slaughter (1991), and Slaughter (1991), and the content analysis of Bensimon (1989), Goffman (1974), Tannen (1990), and Tierney (1983), I will attempt here to deconstruct what these individuals have said by breaking apart their sentence structure so that we might contextualize more fully what the comments suggest. How one defines deconstructionism is notoriously contested; for the purposes of this analysis I call upon the work of Jonathan Culler (1982), who notes, "Deconstruction emphasizes that discourse, meaning, and reading are historical through and through, produced in processes of contextualization, decontextualization, and recontextualization" (p. 129). Essentially, following Derrida, Culler argues that one comes to "meaning" by interpreting the context in which statements are said, deconstructing those contexts and statements, and then "reconstructing" them. In doing so, a deconstructionist assumes that (1) final interpretation is never achieved, and (2) that reinterpretation is always necessary. Accordingly, I offer one possible interpretation of the speakers' comments.

The university president noted: "They have a terrible problem with acculturation."

The statement defined how the speaker perceived the situation. The group that has the "problem" are American Indians. The problem is acculturation and it is not minor; it is a major problem, which the speaker defined as "terrible."

The speaker made this point when asked a "grand tour" open-ended interview question (Spradley, 1979): "Tell me about Native American participation on this campus." The speaker's comment presumably points out knowledge he had with regard to Native American recruitment to and retention in postsecondary education in general, and to his campus in particular. Over 90% of those American Indian students who enter his university will not receive a degree from the institution. The nature of the problem, then, is that Native Americans need to become acculturated to the university in order to persist. Acculturation to the university presumably implies that the Indian student must learn the ways of the White world.

"They grow up without competition, and when they come here to a university whose ethic is achievement and competition, it's tough." The speaker followed his first comment with a consistent line of reasoning. He offered a comparison; Native Americans do not compete, and the university is founded on competition. Indeed, a core "ethic" of the university appears to be "competition."

"Achievement" is related in some way to "competition." That is, the assumption of the speaker was that, to achieve, one must necessarily compete. What one achieves, presumably, is a college degree. Again, drawing upon general and specific data, the speaker knew that Native Americans are not successful; they do not "achieve." The speaker also empathized with American Indians. He recognized the problems they face and pointed out that "it's tough." The speaker, then, assumed that he understood the problems the students face and that the problems are difficult.

The college administrator added: "The major problem is that they have a foot in each culture that draws them back to their roots." This speaker also pointed out that those who have the "problem" are Native Americans, and he believed the same problem existed that the first speaker pointed out. American Indians do not have both feet firmly planted in the university's soil. Their "roots" are in another culture. The problem, then, is that Native Americans have extensive roots, and until they cut those roots, they will not be successful. The speaker also thought that Indian students are involved in two cultures—an Indian culture and an Anglo culture, as experienced at the institution.

"They are drawn back to their own culture and it's a difficult transition to make."

The individual reiterated his first comment. The Indian culture has a serious pull; it "draws" students "back" rather than pushes them forward. To move from one's own culture to a mainstream university was seen as a "transition" and, again, it is a "difficult" or terrible transition to make. To attend a mainstream institution requires that an individual move from one world to another—move from the Native American culture to the Anglo culture. Presumably, such movement propels students forward.

"It's a real problem that's not easy for us to solve." The speaker concluded by objectifying American Indian students—they have become the problem—and the realization that the problem is a difficult one. The problem is also "real"; unlike some problems that mask other concerns, the speaker implied that he has been able to define the problem precisely. However, the problem is like a puzzle; the solution will not be easy.

The individuals who will solve the problem were identified as "us." Inasmuch as the speaker was a senior White male administrator at a mainstream university, we can reasonably presume that the problem's solution lies in the hands of similar White male administrators. At a minimum, the answers will be found by "us"—university administrators—and not "them"—American Indian students.

Analyzing the Discourse

The comments of both speakers reinforce the theoretical argument of the social integrationists. As Tinto (1975) has pointed out, college is a transition where a student leaves his or her past community:

> College students are, after all, moving from one community or set of communities, most typically those of the family and local high school, to another, that of the college. Like other persons in the wider society, they too must separate themselves, to some degree, from past associations in order to make the transition to eventual incorporation in the life of the college. (p. 94)

Thus, social integrationists have hypothesized that success in college is contingent upon an individual's ability to become academically and socially integrated into the life of the institution, a process that is predicated in part on the individual's ability to separate from previous communities. To use Tinto's Durkheimian formulation, the implicit assumption is that Native

Americans will need to undergo a cultural suicide of sorts to avoid an intellectual suicide.

Because discourse is never fixed and determined, a number of alternative possibilities exist with regard to how one might see minority participation in academe. For example, rather than defining Native Americans as the ones who have the "problem," we might think of the institutions as having the "problem." Indeed, the "problem" might be defined not as a group's lack of "acculturation" but as an institution's inability to operate in a multicultural world. From a Native American perspective, a "problem" might be defined as the university's "ethic of achievement and competition" as opposed to an ethic of cooperation and willingness to work together.

Instead of implying that being "drawn back" to one's own culture is a shortcoming, one might accentuate that ripping one away from his or her native culture is detrimental and harmful. Rather than think of college as an abrupt transition from one world to another, we might try to conceptualize college life as reinforcing and incorporating what one has learned from one's extended family.

And, of course, regardless of how one defines a problem, it is possible to think of the "solution" lying not in the hands of the powerful, but in the hands of those who are most centrally involved in the issue. Rather than objectify Native Americans as the problem, one might point out that institutional racism and the mind-set of the powerful is the "real problem."

Discussion

My point in this chapter has been to highlight the conceptual inadequacy of current theories of student participation. I have concentrated on Tinto's research primarily because his work is the most widely accepted and sophisticated analysis we have. And as the statements from the college officials highlight, the theoretical formulations of social integrationists are enacted in the words and actions of college administrators. My assumption here is that theory does inform practice and that many of the recent attempts by college officials pertaining to minority recruitment and retention have utilized researchers' findings to solve the "problem." However, the solutions have been inadequate, precisely because we are asking the wrong questions.

From the argument advanced in this chapter, the challenge for researchers is twofold. First, we need to use different theoretical models from those that insist upon an integrative framework that assumes an individualist stance. In effect, Tinto's use of culture as a framework has moved us in the right direction, but he has not gone far enough. Critical and feminist theories are but two examples of the kinds of models we might find useful as we reconceptualize student participation in academe. The recent works of Holland and Eisenhart (1990), and others (Tierney, 1989, 1992; Weis, 1985), are examples of how such theories may be employed to analyze academe.

The second challenge relates to how decision makers might be able to use these more recent theoretical developments. The changes required are not just theoretical; as the examples from the administrators demonstrate, theoretical reconceptualizations also need to influence how individuals act. As McLaughlin (1989) has argued,

> Many times, the calls of critical theorists for transformative leadership and transformative intellectualism amount to obfuscating rhetoric which, in over intellectualizing what is wrong with mainstream school practices without identifying what actually teachers and school administrators can do, simply add to the problem. (p. 58)

Thus, we need to go further not only by delineating the scaffolding for critical or feminist theories and the like but also by suggesting how we might employ such theoretical orientations in the daily operations of our institutions. We need to consider how institutionally sponsored interventions function within the variety of different contexts that exist for different issues such as minority student retention.

I am arguing, then, for a radical reorientation of how we conceptualize and, hence, act in the organizational worlds of academe. The task of conceiving different theoretical horizons will enable us not only to offer alternative strategies for developing multicultural environments but also to reconfigure the social conditions of power that give voice to some and silence others. In doing so, we will be moving away from a model of social integration and assimilation and toward a framework of emancipation and empowerment.

References

Astin, A. (1977). *Four critical years: Effects of college on beliefs, attitudes, and knowledge*. San Francisco: Jossey-Bass.

Attinasi, L. C., Jr. (1989). Getting in: Mexican Americans' perceptions of university attendance and the implications for freshman year persistence. *Journal of Higher Education, 60*, 247–277.

Badwound, E. (1990). *Leadership and American Indian values: The tribal college dilemma.* Ph.D. dissertation, The Pennsylvania State University, University Park.

Bean, J. P., & Metzner, B. S. (1985, March). *A conceptual model of nontraditional student attrition.* Paper presented at the annual meeting of the Association for the Study of Higher Education, Chicago, IL.

Benally, H. (1988). Diné philosophy of learning. *Journal of Navajo Education, 6*, 10–13.

Bensimon, E. M. (1989). A feminist reinterpretation of presidents' definitions of leadership. *Peabody Journal of Education, 66*, 143–156.

Cabrera, A. F., Stampen, O. J., & Hansen, W. L. (1990). Explaining the effects of ability to pay on persistence in college. *Review of Higher Education, 13*, 303–336.

Colon, A. (1991). Race relations on campus: An administrative perspective. In P. G. Altbach & K. Lomotey (Eds.), *The racial crisis in American higher education* (pp. 69–88). Albany: State University of New York Press.

Culler, J. (1982). *On deconstruction: Theory and criticism after structuralism.* Ithaca, NY: Cornell University Press.

Durkheim, E. (1951). *Suicide.* (J. A. Spaulding & G. Simpson, Trans.). Glencoe, IL: The Free Press.

Fay, B. (1987). *Critical social science.* Ithaca, NY: Cornell University Press.

Foster, W. (1989). The administrator as a transformative intellectual. *Peabody Journal of Education, 66*, 5–18.

Giroux, H. (1988). Border pedagogy in the age of postmodernism. *Journal of Education, 170*, 162–181.

Giroux, H. (1990). The politics of postmodernism. *Journal of Urban and Cultural Studies, 1*, 5–38.

Goffman, E. (1974). *Frame analysis.* New York: Harper and Row.

Holland, D. C., & Eisenhart, M. A. (1990). *Educated in romance: Women, achievement, and college culture.* Chicago, IL: The University of Chicago Press.

Leach. E. (1968). *International encyclopedia of the social sciences* (Vols. 13–14). New York: Macmillan.

McLaughlin, D. (1989). Power and the politics of knowledge: Transformative leadership and curriculum development for minority language learners. *Peabody Journal of Education, 66*, 41–60.

McNeley, J. P. (1988). A Navajo curriculum in the national context. *Journal of Navajo Life*, 125–136.

Nora, A., Attinasi, L. C., Jr., & Matonak, A. (1990). Testing qualitative indicators of precollege factors in Tinto's attrition model: A community college student population. *Review of Higher Education, 13*, 337–355.

Olivas, M. A. (1982). Indian, Chicano, and Puerto Rican colleges: Status and issues. *Bilingual Review*, *9*, 36–58.

Olivas, M. A. (1983). The Tribally Controlled Community College Assistance Act of 1978: The failure of federal Indian higher education policy. *American Indian Law Review*, *9*, 219–251.

Olneck, M. R. (1990). The recurring dream: Symbolism and ideology in intercultural and multicultural education. *American Journal of Education*, *98*, 147–174.

Padilla, R. V., & Pavel, M. (1989, March). *The role of student advising in academic integration*. Paper presented at the annual meeting of the American Educational Research Association, San Francisco, CA.

Rhoades, G. (1990). Calling on the past: The quest for the collegiate model. *Journal of Higher Education*, *61*, 512–534.

Rhoades, G., & Slaughter, S. (1991). The public interest and professional labor: Research universities. In W. G. Tierney (Ed.), *Culture and ideology in higher education: Advancing a critical agenda* (pp. 187–212). New York: Praeger.

Slaughter, S. (1991). The "official" ideology of higher education: Ironies and inconsistencies. In W. G. Tierney (Ed.), *Culture and ideology in higher education: Advancing a critical agenda* (pp. 59–86). New York: Praeger.

Spady, W. (1970). Dropouts from higher education: An interdisciplinary review and synthesis. *Interchange*, *1*, 64–85.

Spady, W. (1971). Dropouts from higher education: Toward an empirical model. *Interchange*, *2*, 38–62.

Spindler, G., & Spindler, L. (1989). There are no dropouts among the Arunta and Hutterites. In H. T. Trueba, G. Spindler, & L. Spindler (Eds.), *What do anthropologists have to say about dropouts?* (pp. 7–15). New York: Falmer Press.

Spradley, J. P. (1979). *The ethnographic interview*. New York: Holt, Rinehart, and Winston.

Stage, F. K. (1990). Research on college students: Commonality, difference and direction. *Review of Higher Education*, *13*, 249–258.

Tannen, D. (1990). *You just don't understand*. New York: Morrow.

Tierney, W. G. (1983). Governance by conversation: An essay on the structure, function, and communicative codes of a faculty senate. *Human Organization*, *42*, 172–177.

Tierney, W. G. (1989). *Curricular landscapes, democratic vistas: Transformative leadership in higher education*. New York: Praeger.

Tierney, W. G. (1992). *Official encouragement, institutional discouragement: Minorities in academe—The Native American experience*. Norwood, NJ: Ablex.

Tierney, W. G. (1993). The college experience of Native Americans: A critical analysis. In L. Weis & M. Fine (Eds.), *Beyond silenced voices: Class, race, and gender in United States schools* (pp. 309–323). Albany, NY: SUNY Press.

Tinto, V. (1975). Dropout from higher education: A theoretical synthesis of recent research. *Review of Educational Research, 45,* 89–125.

Tinto, V. (1982). Limits of theory and practice in student attrition. *Journal of Higher Education, 53,* 687–700.

Tinto, V. (1987). *Leaving college: Rethinking the causes and cures of student attrition.* Chicago: The University of Chicago Press.

Turner, V. (1977). *The ritual process: Structure and anti-structure.* Ithaca, NY: Cornell University Press.

Van Gennep, A. (1960). *The rites of passage* (M. Vizedon & G. Caffee, Trans.). Chicago: University of Chicago Press.

Weis, L. (1985). *Between two worlds.* Boston: Routledge & Kegan Paul.

Wright, B., & Tierney, W. G. (1991). American Indians in higher education: A history of cultural conflict. *Change, 23,* 11–18.

6

ORGANIZATIONAL SOCIALIZATION IN HIGHER EDUCATION

A fact is like a sack which won't stand up when it is empty. In order that it may stand up, one has to put into it the reason and sentiment which have caused it to exist.

—Luigi Pirandello, *Six Characters in Search of an Author*

S ocialization is a concept that is much discussed but frequently misunderstood. On the one hand, the research literature is replete with taken-for-granted definitions of socialization; on the other, institutional administrators often eschew discussions of socialization as a waste of time in comparison to their attempts to solve the myriad problems currently faced by colleges and universities. In this chapter I advance an alternative view of socialization and highlight the importance of utilizing this view for restructuring college and university life.

More specifically, I take issue with many of the common assumptions we share about organizational socialization. In so doing, I suggest that socialization is of fundamental importance with regard to many of the most pressing issues that confront academic administrators and faculty. The national conversations that have begun, for example, about the nature of faculty roles in academic and public life inevitably relate to socialization and culture. In particular, I focus on socialization processes that involve tenure-track faculty

This chapter originally appeared as Tierney, W. G. (1997). Organizational socialization in higher education. *The Journal of Higher Education, 68*(1), 1–16.

in four-year colleges and universities. This chapter is anchored in a two-year study of promotion and tenure based on interviews of over 300 individuals—junior faculty, department chairs, tenure review committee chairs, and senior academic administrators. To be sure, the specific tenure processes vary dramatically from institution to institution; nevertheless, these processes are similar enough across institutional types to enable us to propose a schema for how we might think about organizational socialization and how we might develop policies that contribute to the successful socialization of faculty into the academy.

As a beginning point, we need to consider the nature of the organizational culture in which individuals are socialized. Obviously, a culture whose values and goals are outdated or inconsistent with the world of the 21st century is not necessarily a culture for which we want to socialize new recruits. Accordingly, I first critique previous concepts of socialization as they relate to culture and then offer data that delineate an alternative way we might think about how faculty become socialized. I compare and contrast what I call "modern" and "postmodern" versions of culture and socialization and conclude with suggestions for improving the socialization practices of colleges and universities.

Studying Socialization

Background

"Organizational researchers," writes John Van Maanen (1984), "have over-studied relatively harsh and intensive socialization and understudied socialization of the more benign and supportive sort" (p. 238). Dramatic, celebratory rituals, such as Founder's Day, or graduation, or initiation rites of fraternities, afford us one window of understanding how individuals change from one social status to another or how they become incorporated or invested in an institution or discipline. In this regard the organizational literature is full of examples, from army cadets who rise at dawn and conduct drills and marches that demonstrate loyalty to the academy and their unit to various social groups, such as university marching bands and college honor societies, where the members perform hazing rituals on recruits that bond individuals to the group.

Admittedly, such highly visible events surely play some role in organizational socialization, and our concentration on such examples has been helpful in rethinking actual events. Hazing, for example, is no longer officially condoned on college campuses, because whatever bonding might have taken place was outweighed by the physical and emotional trauma that often happened to recruits. However, when we concentrate on such dramatic actions, we overlook the more implicit and processual activities that circumscribe how individuals become socialized to an organization. Virtually no research supports the view that individuals in organizations such as colleges and universities are socialized primarily through major flash points such as a "reality shock" or an abrupt ritualistic transition. Indeed, often our assumptions about socialization in higher education are folk wisdom that we derive from personal experience in our own organization, but we lack empirical data to support these assumptions.

I suggest that we learn a great deal about, and become socialized to, an organization from the less dramatic, ordinary daily occurrences that take place as we go about the normal business of being a professor, student, administrator, or staff member. Such a point is not merely of theoretical interest. At a time when we hear daily calls to reorient the culture of our organizations so that certain values and processes receive higher prominence (e.g., teaching, advising students, service), we need to consider socialization's processes in their entirety, as opposed to limiting ourselves to isolated examples that serve as grand transitional markers from one stage to another. In effect, if we are socializing people to a cultural ethos that we no longer desire, then it is clearly important to understand the underpinnings of socialization so that we might socialize people to different objectives and goals.

In the following I will first discuss a "modernist" view of culture and socialization and then turn to a "postmodern" interpretation. My intent is to contrast modern and postmodern definitions of culture and socialization and, of consequence, raise questions about how we socialize people to the organizational world.

A Modernist Perspective

In higher education, we often speak of socialization as if it were a unitary and rational process embedded in an understandable culture. Culture gets defined as the sum of activities—symbolic and instrumental—that exist in the organization and create shared meaning. The definition of socialization pertains to the successful understanding and incorporation of those activities by the new members of the organization.

Weidman (1989), quoting Brim, stated that socialization is "the process by which persons acquire the knowledge, skills, and dispositions that make them more or less effective members of their society" (p. 293). Dunn, Rouse, and Seff (1994) echoed Weidman by stating that socialization is "the process by which individuals acquire the attitudes, beliefs, values and skills needed to participate effectively in organized social life" (p. 375). Bragg (1976) pointed out that "the socialization process is the learning process through which the individual acquires the knowledge and skills, the values and attitudes, and the habits and modes of thought of the society to which he belongs" (p. 3). In an article on organizational culture, Tierney (1988) defined socialization by asking, "What do we need to know to survive/excel in the organization?" (p. 8). Kirk and Todd-Mancillas (1991) were similarly instrumental in their definition by linking socialization with academic "turning points" in an individual's life (p. 407).

In large part, all of these definitions are more similar than they are dissimilar. Most important, they use as their base Robert Merton's (1957) ideas about socialization within a society and apply them to an organization. Thus, culture is the sum of activities in the organization, and socialization is the process through which individuals acquire and incorporate an understanding of those activities. Culture is relatively constant and can be understood through reason. An organization's culture, then, teaches people how to behave, what to hope for, and what it means to succeed or fail. Some individuals become competent, and others do not. The new recruit's task is to learn the cultural processes in the organization and figure out how to use them.

A modernist framework affords two viewpoints of the culture of an organization. One view mirrors anthropological notions of cultural relativism. The researcher studies culture and socialization in one college and then in another. One culture is not better than another, only different. The goal is to develop a taxonomy of cultures that demonstrates the diversity that exists.

The second modernist view of culture is to find cultures that are aberrant and in need of repair. This view mimics the cultural deficit model of racial and ethnic groups that focused on the deficiencies of particular groups as an explanation for why they were poor, outcast, and so on. One goal of the deficit model is to explain deficiencies in a group so they can be changed. Thus, in modernism we may investigate the socialization processes of an institution and merely observe that there are multiple paths for enabling people to "acquire knowledge," or we may decide that one institution does a poor job of teaching its recruits about itself. Regardless of the view—cultural relativism or cultural deficit—the theoretical underpinnings about how one conceives of culture and socialization are similar: the culture of the organization is coherent and understandable. The modernist task of socialization is for the recruit to learn the culture. To be sure, learning is ongoing; nevertheless, the goal is to incorporate the mores of the organization's culture.

A Postmodern Perspective

Before considering how we might think about culture and socialization within a postmodern framework, it will be helpful if I offer postmodernist concerns with previous definitions of culture and socialization: (1) the modernist assumption is that socialization is a process where people "acquire" knowledge; (2) socialization is viewed as a one-way process in which the initiate learns how the organization works; and (3) socialization is little more than a series of planned learning activities.

On the surface there is a good deal of what we might think of as common sense in these three modernist assumptions. A new faculty member joins a university, for example, and "acquires" the habits that it takes to succeed. In short, he or she "learns the ropes." Similarly, the idea that new people learn old organizational ways usefully assumes that the organization has a culture or set of processes that need to be learned. As such, socialization is a process that pertains primarily to new members of an organization; the new faculty member needs to learn what is expected of him or her with regard to virtually every aspect of the job. By contrast, when a professor becomes a department chair or an administrator, further socialization occurs, but at this stage the individual socializes himself or herself to a role rather than to the entire organization.

The problem with such definitions is that they endorse a rational view of the world in which reality is fixed and understandable, culture is discovered, and the individual holds an immutable identity that awaits organizational imprinting. A different way to think about culture and socialization is based on postmodernism. Although it is beyond the scope of this chapter to present a critique of the strengths and weaknesses of postmodernism, I offer the scaffolding for how I use postmodernism to think about and analyze culture and socialization.

"Postmodernism," Bloland (1995) argues, "points out that totalization hides contradictions, ambiguities, and oppositions and is a means for generating power and control" (p. 525). As opposed to the modernist version, then, culture is not simply the sum of the tasks that occur in the organization. To the contrary, McDermott and Varenne (1995) note, "Being in the world requires dealing with indefinite and unbounded tasks while struggling with the particular manner in which they have been shaped by the cultural process" (p. 337). Culture is the interpretation the organization's participants give to Pirandello's sacks/facts. Such an interpretation of culture offers a portrait of an organization that is much less determined than that of a modernist organization. In effect, culture is "up for grabs" or contestable. To be sure, constraints exist by way of historical and social forces, but multiple possibilities exist to reinscribe culture with alternative interpretations and possibilities.

From a postmodern perspective, then, culture is not waiting "out there" to be discovered and "acquired" by new members. The coherence of an organization's culture derives from the partial and mutually dependent knowledge of each person caught in the process and develops out of the work they do together. Culture is not so much the definition of the world as it is, but rather a conglomeration of the hopes and dreams of what the organizational world might be. Because culture is constantly being re-created, this view of socialization derives from a fundamentally different vantage point than if we assume that ideas, habits, and skills await incorporation by the newcomer. "Life in culture," McDermott and Varenne (1995) remind us,

> is polyphonous and multivocalic; it is made of the voices of many, each one brought to life and made significant by the other, only sometimes by being the same, more often by being different, more dramatically by being contradictory. Culture is not so much a product of sharing, as a product of people hammering each other into shape with the well-structured tools already available. We need to think of culture as this very process of hammering a world. (p. 326)

The modernist assumption that an organization's culture is coherent implies that all people in the culture are the same. A socialization process can be developed that is unitary—one size fits all—and the outcome can be developed on specified outcomes—all candidates need to achieve a particular goal. When we think of culture in this manner, it is easy to see how a culture will have winners and losers, misfits and fully incorporated members. If the purpose of socialization is assimilation, then those who do not learn the correct ways to assimilate will have failed.

However, insofar as socialization is a cultural act, I suggest that it is an interpretive process involved in the creation—rather than the transmittal—of meaning. Culture is not discovered by unchanging recruits. Rather, socialization involves a give-and-take where new individuals make sense of an organization through their own unique backgrounds and the current contexts in which the organization resides. Hazing is a good, albeit overly dramatic, example of my point. In the early 21st century, we think of such actions in a decidedly different manner from individuals who condoned hazing on college campuses 50 years ago. Today it is often considered not only dangerous but also immature and anti-intellectual by a broad spectrum of the college community, whereas bonding of this kind was viewed positively only a generation ago. But even then, all individuals did not interpret the hazing ritual in a similar manner: some recruits saw it as a price one had to pay to join the club and little more, whereas others suffered psychological and/or physical consequences for life.

A postmodern view of organizational culture argues that we ought not think of socialization as a series of social acquisitions that occur in unchanging contexts irrespective of individual and group identity. Individuals do not "acquire" static, sedentary concepts. Socialization is not simply a planned sequence of learning activities where recruits learn one fact and then another. And these "facts," as Pirandello's opening quotation highlights, are open to manifold interpretations.

If socialization is a process through which individuals acquire skills to be "effective members of their society" (Weidman, 1989, p. 293), then we have a unitary view of what it means to be effective. At a minimum we ought to ask ourselves what the implications are when a man or a woman, an Anglo-American, African American, or Latino, a physically challenged or able-bodied individual undergoes socialization. Is socialization nothing more than assimilation—organizational "melting pots"—where successful incorporation means all people march to the same institutional drummer? Do the participants in the organization have any obligation to change, or does the onus of socialization reside strictly with the recruit? Do individuals and groups interpret reality differently?

I focus on these questions with two overriding thoughts: First, what are the implications for an organization that views all of its new recruits from a similar perspective? Second, if we agree that the organizational culture itself has problems, then how might we reconfigure socialization processes? The faculty responses given in the interviews reveal the limitations and problems of today's universities and colleges and raise concerns about the attempt to socialize faculty to organizations that are predicated on problematic assumptions.

Socialization and Tenure Background

One way to understand socialization is from the perspective of those who are being socialized—the recruits. Junior faculty offer a wealth of information about how academe incorporates new members into the academy, and in doing so they teach us about organizational norms, values, and culture. Between 1992 and 1994 I was involved in a project that interviewed over 300 individuals, 90% of whom were junior faculty from eight colleges and universities in the United States. The institutions were located throughout the country and comprised a mixture of public/private and small, medium-sized, and large colleges and universities. Within each institution faculty from different disciplines and colleges were interviewed. For example, at one institution I interviewed junior faculty in the colleges of business, education, and engineering, and faculty in chemistry, biology, history, classics, political science, and Spanish. The intent was to develop as wide a net as possible with regard to junior faculty perceptions of the tenure and promotion process.

The data that I offer here deal specifically with various aspects of faculty work (e.g., teaching, research, service). Van Maanen (1976, 1978, 1984) speaks of socialization occurring in two frames: anticipatory and organizational. Graduate school and job interviews might be considered primary avenues for exploration of anticipatory socialization. Mentoring and the actual yearlong process when a candidate comes up for promotion and tenure are other examples of organizational socialization. Faculty work, however, is the primary arena for organizational socialization to occur in a processual manner, and it highlights the concerns about how individuals learn culture.

Faculty Work

Faculty work for, and are socialized to, academic rewards that are located in a cultural system. In the following section I discuss the intensity of the culture as defined by those who experience it, by the nature of the work, and by the specific units of faculty work—teaching, research, and service.

Pace of Work

The intensity of work during the academic year was characterized similarly by virtually all faculty, regardless of institutional type or discipline: "I work seven days a week," said one individual, "and I mean seven days a week." A second person said, "I take Friday afternoons off—they're for myself, and I get Sunday mornings for my family. Other than that, I work every day." "I get up by five so I can write," commented a third person, "and then I get to work by eight and stay here until about seven." Another person added, "I always leave the office by six so I can have dinner with my family, but once the kids get to sleep, I probably work another two hours. I have to. I have no choice." Across the sample, over three fourths of the faculty commented that they worked at least three nights a week, and more than 90% said they worked for more than four hours at least one day during the weekend.

For women faculty, working long hours was also a way of demonstrating that they were equally committed to their careers as their male colleagues, and they worked hard to prove their single-mindedness. One woman made the following observation:

> In the first year I noticed how much women faculty talked about how much they worked. It seemed to have a competitive flavor: 'I was up until two in the morning.' 'Well, I was up until three, and I'm on eighty committees, and blah, blah, blah.' I got the sense that the more overworked you were, the better faculty person you were.

In the summer, faculty were involved in different activities, but they were equally busy. "I have taken a week with my wife and child in August," said one fourth-year professor, "but this year and next I can't because of tenure." "I like summer because there are no meetings. I still work every day, but I don't have to work in the evenings as much; that's nice," said another individual. A third person added, "I stay home all summer, but it makes me more neurotic, frankly, because then I feel I have to work all the time. I can't remember a day last summer when I totally just vegged out." A fourth person concurred, but from a different angle: "My office is air conditioned and the students aren't around, so I come in early, put on a pot of coffee, and get to it. The kids are home in the summer, so it's not as convenient to work at home. I actually come here more often in the summer." "Summers are a time when I feel terribly isolated and alone. . . . I need to devise a system of checking in with a few people. . . . I don't labor alone very well," said a man who assumed he worked more effectively when he had colleagues with whom to talk or collaborate on writing projects.

Faculty Effectiveness

Given such observations, one may well wonder about the efficiency and nature of faculty work. Perhaps faculty are simply inefficient, and part of socialization is learning how to make better use of their time. It also may be that every professional works as hard as the faculty portrayed themselves as working. Perhaps the engineer or businessperson has a similarly fast-paced work life. As one individual lamented, "I'm not a factory worker. This isn't a nine-to-five job. I guess most people would say they like the freedom of faculty life, but it's a weird freedom, isn't it? The freedom to work all the time." A second person made a similar point: "Everything I do is time-consuming. If you grade papers the way you're supposed to, it takes time. They need to see your comments. And my research, my writing is not something I just sit down and type out and I'm done. I have to think, think, think." Another person added, "When I'm in my lab, I can't force results. Sure, there are ways I've learned to be more efficient, but experiments and ideas are not just putting things together. It's messy." A final observation comes from a faculty member who thinks of himself as primarily a researcher:

> It's funny. I'm paid to do my research. I spend lots of time at it. But I enjoy working with students, and I make myself as available as possible to them. I even hold some office hours on Saturday mornings because I know there won't be interruptions. I have my grad students over to my house all the time. I have no time for myself, and sometimes that causes troubles at home. I've got to find a balance.

A comparative perspective on the pace of work in other professions was provided by many faculty members in business, engineering, or the sciences who previously had been in industry or business. Interestingly, virtually everyone said they worked harder and spent longer hours in their academic positions. "There's no comparison," said one person. "I worked a lot in my last job, sure, but it was not like this." Another person went a step further: "My work is never-ending here, and the pace is relentless. I don't know if I can keep at it, and I am seriously considering returning to industry. Better hours, better pay." A third person stated, "I had no idea what I was in for. The problem is that you never know how much is enough, and you want to do a good job. If you take yourself seriously, that means you just keep working. At [my business company] I knew when I had done a good job. I'd blow off steam and then start on another project. Not here." A fourth person compared the pace of life to a triathlon:

> I don't know if I am a distance runner, biker, and swimmer. I feel like I'm asked to do everything at once and all the time. At work I had one job, one task, and maybe one on the drawing boards. Here, you have one project going, one in planning, one or two you're writing grants for, and the constant submission/revision of articles. Then there are the students. My graduate students line up outside the door, the undergraduates want their exams back, and somebody's always in crisis. And then there's the service side, where you're asked to sit on committees. Who can do all this? Whoever thinks faculty life is the leisurely pursuit of knowledge should follow me around for a while.

Teaching

Junior faculty also tend to segment their lives into separate domains of teaching, research, and service. "I'm not good at giving tests," admitted one assistant professor, "and yes, I know there's an instructional development center on campus. After tenure, I'll probably go there. I don't have time now." "I heard of one person who was told her teaching scores were too high," said another untenured faculty member. "If your scores are too high, it means you're spending too much time on teaching." "I like to teach," commented a third person, "but it's not valued." A fourth person said, "I'm a perfectionist, and the system doesn't like it. I'm an okay teacher. I get good scores, but I could be better; but if I spent my time improving, I wouldn't get tenure."

In small institutions, where teaching is usually the most salient activity, a professor's accessibility to students is one of the many tacit forms of judging whether a new professor embodies desirable qualities. A male professor at a liberal arts college said, "As an undergraduate I never would have walked up to a professor's office and just knocked on the door and expected that professor to drop everything and sit and talk to me, but that is the almost uniform expectation here." "I started off being resistant," said another, "I set specific hours, I would not leave my door open—but when students wrote in their evaluations 'the professor is not available'—I began to change my attitude and have tried to adapt to the culture of the college."

Research

A young male professor at a major research university who admitted to "especially liking undergraduate teaching," said, "It was clear in my mind from things that were said in the interview that research came first, far and away, and as long as I held up my end of the research, if I wanted to be a good teacher too, that was okay." He added that the "research culture" came through in comments, such as, "you don't want to teach undergraduates," "students are a nuisance," and "constant talk about research, research goals, and research needs, and very little about teaching."

"What does it take to get tenure," asked one person. "That's the million-dollar question. Standards change, and you never know how many articles you need." Another person commented, "Everybody talks about it. Someone gets published, and you feel sort of good for the person but frantic for yourself." "I have twenty articles in refereed journals," said another individual, "but people keep telling me I need a book. The dean wants a book."

In general, faculty at every type of institution enjoyed research, although they tended to steer clear of groundbreaking work because it took too long. They needed to write articles, and in the interest of accumulating publications, an individual could not devote years to a project that might not yield results. "I want to get tenure," said one, "and that makes me risk averse. I could go down one road that might lead to a big breakthrough in my field, but it also might lead nowhere. So I go for little results that get me publications." Another person said, "They want me to get published in journals that have low acceptance rates, so that says to me, play it safe."

Service

If research seemed the most important activity of faculty work, the least valued was service. Nevertheless, the expectations for service varied more than any other domain. With service, some faculty were not expected to do anything; others were called on repeatedly. At a small institution, for example, one person explained, "I am on about six committees, and two of them are in my department. Two are for the school, and two more are all-college." Another person complained, "You just get put on them from the vice president's office. It's like you have to take your turn."

Everyone agreed that service did not count in any meaningful sense when a candidate was being considered for tenure. One needed to show that he or she was at least minimally involved in the affairs of the department, but not much more. However, service also provided a way for senior faculty to form opinions about junior faculty and, in this sense, it held symbolic importance. "My department chair told me I should get on college-wide committees," said one individual, "because that's the way faculty in the other departments get to know you." "It's not a good idea," clarified one department chair, "for a younger person to stay hidden away." "Service is hard to evaluate when we go over someone's files," added another full professor, "but it's also the only time, probably, that somebody in another department has had to meet the person or know what he's done."

What are we to make of these snapshots of faculty socialization and work? I elaborate on three data points for discussion: (1) junior faculty spend long hours trying to meet multiple responsibilities; (2) the tasks set for them—teaching, research, and service—are often ill defined and poorly evaluated; and (3) an individual's activity is often devoid of any overriding sense of institutional purpose or identity.

Discussion

Background

One point these interviews underscore is the value and import of looking at the implicit factors of socialization rather than the flash points that Van Maanen noted were overstudied. With few exceptions the participants did not speak of presidential speeches, convocations, or intensive introductory training sessions as ways in which they learned about the organization. Instead, they emphasized that the goals for tenure were unclear: they knew they needed to "produce"—to be a triathlete, one person said—and that the work took a phenomenal amount of time. They learned the pace of work, what was important and what was not, by being involved in the microscopic aspects of the culture of their organizations.

Most individuals pointed out that they had personal preferences—some liked research more than teaching and others teaching more than research—but no one spoke of a deep, embedded ethos for a particular value at their institution. To be sure, some of the interviewees expressed very clearly that their institution had a "culture of research" or that students were considered a "nuisance," but such pronouncements fall far short of conveying a belief in an overriding organizational saga that might be found in a distinctive college (Clark, 1970). Grand markers that conveyed institutional meaning were absent, as were explicit, consistent messages on a more intimate level about what really mattered.

A Modernist Interpretation

In many respects the modern and postmodern definitions that have been provided offer a high degree of consistency with the data. One way to interpret the data is to say that the struggle for the individuals who were being socialized involved "acquiring" specific "skills," "attitudes," and "knowledge." The respondents did not know how to manage their time and thus spent a good deal of effort acquiring the skills necessary to juggle the multiple demands of teaching, committee work, and writing for publication. Many of the quotes highlight the thoughts of individuals who have bought into a system that demands evening and weekend work if they are to succeed.

Even though their tasks were ill defined, these new faculty members seemed to accept that the role of faculty life required a high degree of internal definition about how they were doing. One respondent, for example, suggested that junior faculty spend time on a college-wide committee, not because they were interested or committed to the goals, but because they had internalized the attitudes of what it takes to be a good faculty member. Others had learned that high teaching evaluations were not as important as publications or that being "good enough" at teaching was sufficient; consequently, they were not spending as much time as they would have liked working on lesson plans and other teaching techniques. Thus, individuals were able to subsume personal inclinations in favor of the modernist goal of assimilating to the culture to which they were being socialized.

Also consistent with the modernist perspective is the participants' inability to express any clear sense of institutional belonging or ethos. If cultures are not unique, and individuals interpret cultures similarly, then the data support a view of socialization as the process of acquisition by new, similarly minded recruits. If individuals are not able to socialize themselves so that they fit into the culture, then they fail. The modernist finds in the interview results supportive data for the notion that individuals think they have no control over their lives and that they are unsure of what the goals of the organization are or of what they must do to succeed (as defined by achieving tenure). To the extent that individuals are able to fit themselves into such a culture, they succeed.

A Postmodern Perspective

A postmodern way of thinking about the data is to accept the veracity of what the respondents have said, but to think of ways the outcomes might be altered. Must we have organizations where people feel that the pace is helter-skelter? Is it necessary that individual preferences—teaching as opposed to research, for example—be subjugated to cultural norms? Does service have to play a purely political/symbolic role, or are there alternative configurations? And, finally, is there some institutional genetic predisposition in academic organizations against clear goals that bond people together?

An organization's culture is not internally coherent to all individuals. People are not all alike, and their joining together in an organization suggests that they are involved in the creation—not the discovery or the duplication—of culture. Accordingly, one socialization format does not fit everyone; each individual brings to an organization a unique background and insights, and the challenge lies in using these individual attributes to build the culture of the organization rather than have recruits fit into predetermined norms (Tierney, 1993).

One radical interpretation might be that we have a postmodern culture operating within a modernist framework: conflict and discontinuities exist because people do not know what is expected of them. Of consequence, they fall back on their own interpretations of how to fit within the culture. Yet such an interpretation is unpersuasive if the outcome is assimilation; ultimately, the recruits learn how to teach, work with students, and participate in the community according to the implicit mores of the organization. My point here is to suggest that postmodernism highlights the inherent contradictions that exist within modernist frameworks so that we might be able to develop academic communities that honor difference rather than assimilation.

Goals may be both clear and multiple. It is surely possible to make clearer to an individual what he or she needs to do to succeed. It is equally possible to create an organizational community that uses the idea of excellence and difference, rather than similarity, as its overriding ethos. Such a suggestion is particularly important in a world that is increasingly characterized as permeated by technological and communications breakthroughs that enable, indeed demand, that an organization's participants work toward innovation and change rather than the status quo.

Modernist assumptions highlight a structure in need of modest changes. The data afford views of individuals who conceivably would benefit from a system that might invent various forms of assimilatory processes. That is, various department chairs might benefit from training in how to better inculcate recruits into the culture of the organization. Clearer forms of evaluation might create a more straightforward socialization process. There are multiple discrete acts that would improve the manner in which recruits are socialized to the organization's culture from the modernist perspective. Such suggestions are similar to recommendations that culture of poverty theorists might make when they encounter a culture that is deviant and needs repair.

I argue, however, that at a time when commentary consistently speaks about the need for the overhaul of academe and the manner in which we academics conduct our work, we develop a different way of diagnosing organizational action, culture, and socialization. Postmodernism does not simply suggest that we accept the existence of discontinuities and learn to survive, but, rather, that we deal with the uncertainties and conflicts the data point out as inherent in postmodern organizations by devising a strategy to orchestrate action.

"Learning organizations" and "knowledge-creating companies" are predictions of one kind of institution necessary for the 21st century. Peter Senge (1990), who popularized learning organizations in his book, *The Fifth Discipline*, described them as places "where people continually expand their capacity to create the results they truly desire; where new and expansive patterns of thinking are nurtured" (p. 1). David Garvin (1993) has suggested that a learning organization is an organization skilled at creating, acquiring, and transferring knowledge and at modifying its behavior to reflect new knowledge and insights (p. 80).

Such organizations work from frameworks that accept difference and discontinuity, rather than similarity and continuity. Clearly, then, if we desire an organization that modifies rather than reinforces behavior, we need a schema of socialization that allows for creativity and difference to flourish rather than one that asks its members to become incorporated into a unitary mind-set. Instead of tinkering with a system such as promotion and tenure, a system that socializes people to a unified view of organizational culture, we need to be mindful of alternative conceptions of culture and socialization.

If we study culture from the perspective argued for here, the subject shifts from *them*—the recruits—to *us*—those who establish organizational norms. Rather than try to socialize people to static norms, we reconsider what it means to the organization when new individuals are included. To be sure, individuals change when they enter a new workplace, but from the perspective argued for here, an equally dramatic change also needs to be considered by the current participants in the organization. Indeed, rather than seek individuals who fit the organization, a learning organization seeks to expand what we mean by organizational fit. Such an approach requires rethinking how we have structured organizational rewards and sanctions and acknowledging that when an individual is socialized, this individual is participating in the re-creation, rather than merely the discovery, of a culture.

References

Bloland, H. G. (1995). Postmodernism and higher education. *Journal of Higher Education, 66*(5), 521–559.

Bragg, A. K. (1976). *The socialization process in higher education.* Washington, DC: American Association of Higher Education.

Clark, B. R. (1970). *The distinctive college: Antioch, Reed, and Swarthmore.* Chicago: Aldine.

Dunn, D., Rouse, L., & Seff, M. A. (1994). New faculty socialization in the academic workplace. In J. C. Smart (Ed.), *Higher education: Theory and research* (Vol. 10, pp. 374–413). New York: Agathon.

Garvin, D. A. (1993). Building a learning organization. *Harvard Business Review, 71*(4), 78–91.

Kirk, D., & Todd-Mancillas, W. R. (1991). Turning points in graduate student socialization: Implications for recruiting future faculty. *Review of Higher Education, 14*(3), 407–422.

McDermott, R., & Varenne, H. (1995). Culture as disability. *Anthropology and Education Quarterly, 26*(3), 324–348.

Merton, R. K. (1957). *Social theory and social structure.* Glencoe, IL: The Free Press.

Senge, P. M. (1990). *The fifth discipline: The art and practice of the learning institution.* New York: Doubleday.

Tierney, W. G. (1988). Organizational culture in higher education: Defining the essentials. *Journal of Higher Education, 59*(1), 2–21.

Tierney, W. G. (1993). *Building communities of difference: Higher education in the twenty-first century.* Westport, CT: Bergin & Garvey.

Van Maanen, J. (1976). Breaking in: Socialization to work. In R. Dubin (Ed.), *Handbook of work, organization, and society* (pp. 67–130). Chicago: Rand McNally.

Van Maanen, J. (1978). People processing: Strategies of organizational socialization. In R. W. Allan & L. W. Porter (Eds.), *Organizational influence processes* (pp. 18–36). Glenview, IL: Scott Foresman.

Van Maanen, J. (1984). Doing new things in old ways: The chain of socialization. In J. L. Bess (Ed.), *College and university organization: Insights from the behavioral sciences* (pp. 211–247). New York: New York University Press.

Weidman, J. C. (1989). Undergraduate socialization: A conceptual approach. In J. C. Smart (Ed.), *Higher education: Handbook of theory and research* (Vol. 5, pp. 289–322). New York: Agathon.

7

MODELS OF MINORITY COLLEGE GOING AND RETENTION

Cultural Integrity Versus Cultural Suicide

I n 1970, the Carnegie Commission on Higher Education predicted that it would not be necessary for colleges and universities in the year 2000 to provide compensatory education programs or to struggle over flexible criteria for admissions and grading. Though one might admire the boldness and hopes of such an assertion, the reality of the prediction is one of dreams deferred, if not denied, for those who have not had equal access to postsecondary education. Although more people attend a postsecondary institution today than at any other time in history, not all high school graduates are academically prepared for success in college. Large discrepancies, determined by income and race/ethnicity, continue to persist. Broadly stated, the poor and working classes are less likely to attend college than are the wealthy. Black, Hispanic, and Native American students are less likely to attend a postsecondary institution and to attain a degree than are their European American and Asian American counterparts.

Since the Carnegie Commission made its hopeful prediction in 1970, postsecondary institutions and other related agencies have tried a variety of remedies to increase college participation among low-income and ethnic minority youth. Several significant and far-reaching strategies were devised and employed to increase postsecondary educational opportunities and attendance by underrepresented populations. State and federal governments

This chapter originally appeared as Tierney, W. G. (1999). Models of minority college-going and retention: Cultural integrity versus cultural suicide. *The Journal of Negro Education*, 68(1), 80–91.

stepped in to provide the financial assistance necessary for students from low-income families to attend college in the form of grants and loans. Similarly, minority students who had been discriminated against in the past, or who needed additional consideration to be admitted to a college or university, merited a systematic plan—affirmative action—to ensure equal opportunity. However, as we begin the 21st century, equal access to postsecondary opportunities has not yet been achieved by low-income and minority youth. Affirmative action, if not in danger of outright elimination, came under attack or has been banned in some states, and financial aid lags behind what it once was.

Although I support the basic premises of affirmative action and financial aid (Tierney, 1996, 1997), my intent in this chapter is not to debate the merits of these policies for those who need them most. Even if these approaches were firmly in place, low-income and minority youth would still lag far behind their counterparts in college participation. It is thus not hard to conclude that alternative policies ought to be used if access and equity are to remain goals for society. Though they are surely not a panacea, existing alternatives offer an avenue for increasing college access for low-income and minority youth. However, as Perna and Swail (1998) have noted, very little is known about the status or success of these options from national, state, or local perspectives.

Accordingly, this chapter first delineates a theoretical framework for thinking about college preparation programs that utilizes the work of French sociologist Pierre Bourdieu (1977, 1986). It then describes one such program, the Neighborhood Academic Initiative (NAI) that I studied from 1997 to 1999. Last, it offers a "cultural integrity" model that might be used to develop other such programs and thereby increase minority students' access to and participation and retention in postsecondary education.

College Access and Retention: Assessing Traditional Notions of Capital and Identity

Financial Aid

As suggested, one significant assumption about the relationship between college access and retention has been that financial aid enables youth to participate in college. A panoply of research has been done that addresses issues pertaining to economic assistance for those who cannot, or perceive they cannot, afford college. Hossler, Braxton, and Coopersmith (1989), St. John (1990), and McPherson and Shapiro (1998), for example, have all touched on the effects of financial aid on student choices about whether to attend college.

An underlying assumption for at least a generation has held that low-income and, increasingly, working-class youth either are not able to afford or believe they cannot afford the costs of college. The policy-related response has been that more economic support is needed to enable such students to go to college. Although the importance of financial aid as a means of improving access to postsecondary opportunities should not be downplayed, Gladieux and Swail's (1998) assertion deserves highlighting here. As they conclude: "Everyone knows that financial aid is not enough, that to equalize college opportunities for the poor requires more fundamental, complementary strategies" (p. 11). Financial aid, albeit important, is not a sufficient remedy to independently resolve the dilemma of college student access and retention.

Academic and Social Integration

A second pervasive and implicit assumption about college access is grounded in Tinto's (1987) theory of college student departure. According to Braxton, Sullivan, and Johnson (1997), Tinto has developed a model explicating the reasons for college student attrition that has reached "near paradigmatic status" (p. 108). Although the intent of this chapter is not to critique this model with regard to its primary focus on retention, Tinto makes crucial assumptions regarding what must be done to prepare students for academic life in college preparatory classes. These assumptions about academic life have influenced subsequent theories about how to prepare adolescents for that life.

Tinto bases his model of college student retention on the work of Durkheim (1951) and Van Gennep (1960). As I have noted in previous work (Tierney, 1992, 2000), Durkheim postulates that the cause of suicide in Western societies is the failure of certain individuals to integrate themselves into larger societal structures such as the church, the state, or the family. Van Gennep's contribution to Tinto's model relates to the former's contention that different groups of people participate in initiation rites that allow group members to move from one status (i.e., adolescence) to another (i.e., adulthood). Tinto used these theorists' ideas to develop his model of college student departure, which views college as an initiation ritual, with the success of the initiates—that is, the students—being dependent upon the degree to which they are able to integrate into the social and academic life of postsecondary institutions.

The implications of Tinto's model for college preparation programs are quite significant. If one agrees that a theoretical basis for college student attrition is dependent upon "the roots of individual departure" (Tinto, 1987, p. 37), then one focuses on the individual. On the other hand, if one asserts, as Tinto does, that adolescents must "physically as well as socially dissociate themselves from the communities of [their] past" to become fully incorporated into the life of the academy (p. 96), then a particular conception of local community and culture arises. Further, if one focuses, like Tinto, on "social and intellectual membership in the academic and social communities of the college" (p. 109), a particular view of success arises.

Tinto's model raises both theoretical and practical concerns. On a theoretical level, Van Gennep's anthropological model never assumed that a rite of passage was undertaken by individuals from one culture seeking initiation into a foreign culture. Navajo adolescents, for example, undergo rites of passage within Navajo culture; they do not undergo Apache or European American initiation rituals. To a large extent, African American adolescents' cultural backgrounds differ in significant ways from the middle- and upper-class Eurocentric cultural framework upon which U.S. postsecondary education is based. Yet, according to Tinto's model, these youth undergo rites of passage framed within this "foreign" culture.

Further, as Spindler and Spindler (1989) note, rites of passage are always successful. Referring to the Arunta people of Australia, they state: "All of the initiates succeed, none fail. . . . The whole operation of the initiation school is managed to produce success. To fail to initiate the young successfully is unthinkable" (p. 10). Obviously, the same cannot be said for Black youth on White campuses. For these young people, the "initiation" of college is frequently unsuccessful. Thus, Tinto's model marks a radical departure from what Van Gennep theoretically posits about initiation rites.

Additionally, on a practical level, the Durkheimian idea of suicide paints a disturbing portrait for students of color on predominantly White campuses. Tinto's notion is that college initiates must undergo a form of cultural suicide, whereby they make a clean break from the communities and cultures in which they were raised and integrate and assimilate into the dominant

culture of the colleges they attend. To the extent that they integrate and assimilate, Tinto contends, college students will be successful. Conversely, if
they fail to assimilate, they will fail at college.

Taken together, the concepts of financial aid and academic and social
integration suggest a quite specific model that college preparation programs
might follow. The traditional assumptions are that (1) individuals need economic capital to be able to succeed in college; (2) they also need to be individually oriented; and (3) they need the requisite skills to assimilate into the
academic culture of the institution. In other words, not only are students'
cultural backgrounds irrelevant to their successful collegiate experience, if
students are to succeed in college, those backgrounds must be discarded in
favor of the dominant cultures of their institutions. Moreover, if an initiate/
student fails, the blame falls on the individual, not the institution.

Cultural Considerations

One view of capital pertains to economic ideas. One interpretation of identity pertains to a singular, cohesive self, absent of culture. An alternative
viewpoint, however, uses the idea of culture as the theoretical framework for
defining capital and identity. Nonetheless, culture is an elusive term that
demands definition. It is a set of symbolic processes, ideologies, and socio-
historical contexts that are situated in an arena of struggle, contestation, and
multiple interpretations. As McDermott and Varenne (1995) note, "Culture
is not a property of individuals-as-conditioned" (p. 344). Rather than being
a homogenous entity, culture is a site of production in which individuals
engage not only in efforts to achieve the goals of a group or organization but
also in the processes used to achieve those goals. Researchers investigate the
properties and interpretations of different cultures to come to terms, for example, with why some succeed and others fail.

Thus, a cultural view of issues of college access and retention interprets
the world differently from those notions that contend that an individual's
success or failure in college is dependent upon singular variables such as financial need. Rather than view the academic world as a place into which
students need to fit and assimilate or face intellectual suicide, this explanation views the academy as ripe for reinterpretation and restructuring. Not
only must students fit into the academic culture, but educational organizations must also accommodate for and honor students' cultural differences.

Bourdieu's (1986) work is particularly instructive in this regard. Bourdieu coined the term "cultural capital" to refer to the set of linguistic and cultural competencies individuals usually inherit and sometimes learn (p. 246). However, as McDonough (1997) notes, "cultural capital is precisely the knowledge the elites value yet schools do not teach" (p. 9). Bourdieu's assumption is that individuals from the middle and upper classes inherit cultural capital through their families and neighborhoods. As a result, they learn from an early age that admission to college is not a choice but a preordained conclusion. The question for them is not whether they *should* go to college, or if they can afford it, but *which* college they will attend. In this light, the culture in which individuals reside determines whether they have the cultural capital to attend college.

Bourdieu (1986) further postulates that cultural capital exists in three forms: embodied, objectified, and institutionalized. In the embodied state, capital pertains to dispositions of mind and body. Embodied capital is experienced as "high" culture or engagement with traditional notions of art and cultivation, and involvement with formal definitions of aesthetics and the like, such as might be the case of a patron of the arts. Museums are examples of sites where one finds and obtains embodied capital.

In the objectified state, capital refers to cultural goods; however, it is not merely the ownership of material goods, as simple ownership takes little more than economic capital. Instead, objectified capital refers to the ability to use and enjoy that which one owns. An individual who cherishes a particular sculpture or painting, for example, might also be seen as having objectified capital.

In the institutionalized state, capital refers to the license that an institution or governing body confers on individuals who have achieved a societally sanctioned goal or status. Institutionalized capital is best exemplified by a college degree, which suggests that an individual has acquired the capital necessary to assume a particular position in society. Obviously, the institution from which one acquires such capital increases its worth. For example, the institutionalized capital conferred with a degree from Harvard University is worth more than that of a degree from a community college.

If one looks at cultural capital from a systemic rather than an individual perspective, then Bourdieu's (1977) concept of "habitus" as "a system of lasting, transposable dispositions which, integrating past experiences, functions at every moment as a matrix of perceptions, appreciations and actions" is especially salient (pp. 82–83). More simply put, habitus is the set of perceptions individuals have of their environment. The strength of Bourdieu's concept is that it enables analysis of how micro-practices are linked to broader social and cultural forces to reproduce inequities. One critique of the concept, however, is that habitus may be seen as a rigid and objectified social construct against which individuals are helpless to react and create conditions for change and empowerment (Varenne & McDermott, 1998). From such a perspective, individuals are seen not as agents struggling within cultures but as mere actors trapped in modern-day cages that encapsulate their experience and interpretation and lead to the reproduction of their social and economic conditions.

Bourdieu's idea of cultural capital is helpful when considering minority student access and retention on predominantly White campuses. It enables one to better critique Gladieux and Swail's (1998) contention that financial aid alone is insufficient to provide all students with equal access to postsecondary opportunities. Indeed, the construct also enables policy makers and analysts to communicate about what students need if they are to gain access to and graduate from postsecondary institutions. Minority students often need financial aid to pursue their educational goals after high school, but they also need to acquire the cultural capital that majority students typically inherit. They need the embodied capital required to enable them to interpret and decode different cultural objects, and they need objectified capital such as access to books and application forms and the ability to score well on standardized tests. Last but not least, they need institutionalized capital such as a bachelor's degree.

However helpful such notions of cultural capital are, when they are coupled with the idea of habitus, they may portend that change is impossible. If one interprets Tinto's model as suggesting that minority college students need to shed their cultural heritage in order to succeed in school, then the opposite interpretation might be applied to Bourdieu's habitus model: the ability to shed one's cultural heritage is impossible. The concept of cultural integrity can help to elucidate this.

In previous work, I defined cultural integrity in the context of schooling as those school-based programs and teaching strategies that engage students' racial/ethnic backgrounds in a positive manner toward the development of more relevant pedagogies and learning activities (Tierney & Jun, 2001). Deyhle (1995) has also demonstrated the importance of cultural integrity for academic performance. Her study noted that Native American children who were secure in their traditional culture and identity—that is, those who refused to accept either assimilation or cultural rejection—were more academically successful in school than were their culturally insecure peers. Such students thrived academically while maintaining their identities as Navajos within their communities of origin. Similarly, in a study of successful African American high school students, O'Connor (1997) points out that while the high-achieving Black girls in her study "shared many of the same background characteristics," they also "expressed a high degree of racial consciousness, and, through their operation of the Black collective 'we' they each affirmed their affiliation with the African American community" (p. 594). In my own work (Tierney, 1992), I have pointed out that, when minority college students are able to affirm their own cultural identities, their chances for graduation increase. By this, I do not mean to suggest that the mere celebration of minority cultures on college campuses is sufficient to enable individual students of color to overcome any socioeconomic obstacles they may face. However, if postsecondary institutions make concerted and meaningful efforts to affirm these students' cultural identities, they stand to gain increased possibilities for ensuring the latter's success in college—if the structure of the education these students receive also involves a commitment to high academic and social goals and active learning.

The ideas of cultural capital and cultural integrity move educators away from notions that either money or cultural assimilation will resolve the inequitable educational opportunities experienced by large numbers of students of color in the United States. Cultural integrity transfers the problem of educational inequity from the student to the institution and identifies cultural background as an essential element for academic success. Whereas Tinto's model assumes that college students must commit a form of cultural suicide to be academically successful, students from marginalized communities should find ways to have their cultural backgrounds affirmed and honored on their respective campuses. By so doing, the habitus of students who do not have much in the way of economic or traditional modes of cultural capital is less deterministic and more fluid. Such students are thus able to act as social agents and produce the conditions for change and improvements in opportunity.

What might such conditions look like, and how might they function in a college preparatory program? The following section describes a unique and noteworthy program, built on much of the theoretical work discussed here, that attempts to help low-income urban youth of color get into and succeed in college.

The Neighborhood Academic Initiative

My colleague and I conducted a three-year research study that began with an analysis of existing college preparation programs and yielded a taxonomy delineating different approaches to instruction and learning (Tierney & Jun, 2001). The Neighborhood Academic Initiative (NAI) was a central focus of that study. The NAI is a program for low-income urban minority adolescents in grades 7 through 12, whose chances of attending college without financial and other forms of assistance are slim. Housed on the campus of the University of Southern California (USC), this early intervention program focuses on "enhancing the awareness of, and readiness for, college among underrepresented groups early enough in their lives in order to have a positive influence on their educational outcomes" (Perna & Swail, 1998, p. 8).

Since 1990, approximately 40 African American and Hispanic American 7th graders have been chosen annually to participate in the NAI. They are chosen from two inner-city Los Angeles, California, public schools based on two criteria: (1) they must express a willingness to learn that is supported and encouraged by their parents, and (2) they must have a "C" average or above. The vast majority of NAI candidates come from a population that is often defined as "at-risk" according to multiple criteria. That is, most of their families are in the lowest socioeconomic quartile, most come from single-parent families that contain no family members who have attended college, and the majority have changed schools more than twice previously (Horn & Chen, 1998). Although approximately 30% of NAI students who enter the program in the 7th grade drop out of school prior to the 12th grade, the remaining 70% go on to graduate from high school, and 60% of those graduates enroll in four-year colleges. This is a remarkable rate of success, given that the college-going rate for high school students nationally is about 40% (Mehan, Villanueva, Hubbard, & Lintz, 1996) and below 20% locally (Colvin & Sahagun, 1998).

What accounts for the success of NAI students? One touchstone is the promise of tuition remission the program offers to participating students.

USC has made a commitment to ensure that every NAI student who graduates from high school and who meets the requirements for admission to USC receives complete tuition remission upon enrollment. However, as helpful and necessary as such an incentive is, the experience of the NAI program has shown that financial assistance is inadequate if little else is done. The students whom this program serves need not only economic capital but also cultural capital and cultural integrity to reach and succeed in college.

The NAI works from quite different premises than those upon which Tinto's model is based. Rather than viewing the students' families and neighborhoods as impediments to their success, NAI program administrators view these entities as critical agents for creating the conditions for success. A significant portion of NAI staff live in the South Central Los Angeles community in which the program and its participating schools are embedded. Thus, the development among participating students and families of a sense of Bourdieu's embodied and objectified capital occurs—not *despite* the students' families and neighborhoods but *because* of them. Moreover, the NAI uses specific strategies to enhance cultural capital. These strategies are threefold: (1) to develop local contexts; (2) to affirm local definitions of identity; and (3) to create academic capital.

Developing Local Contexts

Implicit in Tinto's model is the assumption that success in college is partly dependent upon Durkheimian notions. That is, students must divorce themselves from their previous relationships—in effect, commit a form of suicide or figuratively "kill off" their former selves—and forge new selves and relationships in order to integrate themselves successfully into collegiate life. The model implicitly suggests that college-bound students need to leave not only their youth behind them but also their cultures (Tierney, 1992). In some respects, such a framework may be particularly helpful for low-income urban minority youth. Families with no members who have gone to college may be irrelevant to the academic process. Neighborhoods that have high rates of unemployment and crime may be not only irrelevant but also harmful to college-bound youth. Indeed, the removal of Native American youth from their families and reservations during the early part of the 20th century was partly based on such beliefs (Wright & Tierney, 1991).

NAI works from the opposite perspective. A central component of the program is that a family member or guardian must be involved in each participating child's learning. Saturday classes for family members begin when the child enters the seventh grade and continues through his or her high school graduation. These classes deal with a broad range of topics, such as how to create a favorable study environment for the student, how to talk about sex with teenagers, and how to complete the paperwork associated with college applications. The assumption behind this extra involvement is that the family and neighborhood are essential elements of learning. As I have pointed out elsewhere (Tierney, 2000; Tierney & Jun, 2001), NAI staff view family members or guardians as neither irrelevant nor harmful to efforts to create the conditions for learning. Instead, they are seen as essential. Thus, the program supports the notion that embodied capital is not only necessary for the youth who will be attending college, but it is necessary for these students' family members as well.

Schools in inner-city neighborhoods are often seen as divorced from the daily worlds of the students and families they serve. NAI staff attempt to renegotiate this viewpoint by hosting seminars and community meetings that show teachers and counselors how to get to know and support the families of their students and, in turn, show families how to get to know and support their children's teachers and counselors. The program's family involvement component also supports and affirms the cultural backgrounds of NAI students. One explicit purpose of this component is to educate family members about their roles and obligations in ensuring that their children succeed in school. An implicit purpose is to provide opportunities that demonstrate that leaving one's community is not necessary for academic success. In effect, NAI students and families learn that students do not need to drop their family, community, or cultural identities to get into and/or be successful in college.

Affirming Local Definitions of Identity

The NAI values interconnectedness. As its staff become increasingly involved with students and their families during the course of each year, the program often moves out of the schools and into the community. NAI administrators, teachers, and counselors work with local church groups, service agencies, and other support networks to ensure that NAI students enjoy a climate conducive to learning. The relationships that staff develop with supporting groups in the local community build on the notion that all students are talents to be developed rather than problems to be solved. Thus, students are not seen as broken or "at risk" but, instead, are viewed as valuable resources for their communities and society at large.

Much of the NAI's programming is based on the assumption that its students will have to confront racism and prejudice during their college experience. To help students prepare for this reality, the program's personnel guidelines insist that as many NAI administrators, teachers, and counselors as feasible share the same cultural and racial/ethnic backgrounds as the students who participate in the program. Although NAI does not discriminate in its hiring practices, this emphasis helps to ensure that program staff operate, as a matter of principle, from a pedagogical perspective that affirms the local cultural identities of NAI students. It also helps NAI accomplish its objective of providing students with suitable role models. As a result, the students are given opportunities to work with and learn from individuals who come from similar backgrounds or who, at the very least, understand and value the importance of cultural integrity.

To affirm the cultural identity of NAI students and families, the program highlights participants' cultural backgrounds and local contexts. As staff attempt to help students understand the role and influence that racism can play in their college experiences, they also make clear that racism is never an excuse for poor grades or test scores. Indeed, they endeavor to show students ways to learn even when they are in classrooms where others may try to stereotype them in a particular way. This approach supports conclusions that O'Connor (1997) has pointed out in her work with low-income African American youth, namely that "immediate experiences and discourses are essential for understanding the variation which exists within historical and structural parameters and how this variation differentially affects students' dispositions toward school" (p. 624). From this perspective, the affirmation of one's cultural identity is a key attribute in overcoming what Steele (1997) defines as *stereotype threat*, or circumstances in which individuals from minority communities are stereotyped in ways that preclude academic success. Thus, the habitus/cultural capital dialectic is acknowledged. However, rather than assuming that habitus is an impenetrable structure that cannot accommodate the needs of minority youth, NAI develops the conditions for capital creation, which, in turn, gets students into college and, ultimately, retains them.

Creating Academic Capital

According to one informant, the NAI is a "loving boot camp." The discipline demanded by the program is framed within the context of the affirmation NAI provides to its participating students and families of who they are and where they come from. NAI administrators, teachers, and counselors have been consistently described by students as people who not only understand the kinds of challenges faced by low-income youth of color but who also believe in those youth. Notwithstanding, if financial aid is not enough, it is also a truism that, for students who attend schools that historically have evidenced low achievement levels and minuscule college-going rates, merely affirming students' identities is likewise insufficient. The NAI thus creates a safe learning environment where the fundamentals are considered essential. Structure, constant attention to detail, and an emphasis on achieving not merely acceptable but excellent results are cornerstones of the program.

NAI students arrive at their classrooms sometimes as early as 6:30 a.m. They take two classes revolving around English and mathematics lessons prior to the start of their regular school day; attend classes on Saturdays and during the summer; and take frequent trips to museums, plays, and other cultural events. NAI teachers give students homework virtually every night. Assignments that are sloppy or handed in late are returned to the student to do over. Students also participate in counseling sessions that are embedded within their NAI classes. When a social or emotional problem arises, on an individual or group level, students typically take a bit of time out of their class activities to discuss it. The assumption is that students should be ready to learn at all times. If something is bothering them, then it is interfering with their learning and should be addressed immediately.

NAI administrators, teachers, and counselors emphasize that graduation from high school is not enough, nor is admission to college sufficient—the acquisition of a college degree is the ultimate goal. In this way, staff highlight for participating students the importance of institutionalized capital and imbue them with a form of cultural capital that middle- and upper-class students take for granted. The program essentially de-tracks students who have been relegated to the margins of academe by virtue of their attendance at inner-city schools. The structure of the program, the affirmation of local contexts, the emphasis on cultural identities—all these aspects amount to a program that has been remarkably successful at getting low-income urban minority students into college.

Yet, how does such a program assist these students once they get into college? Answering this question demands elaboration of a model of cultural integrity.

Intersections: Cultural Identity and Cultural Capital

Most efforts to admit and retain students of color at U.S. colleges and universities take place on the campuses themselves. Affirmative action was once an important tool that helped minority students gain admittance to predominantly White campuses. A panoply of services at colleges and universities has been aimed at increasing retention of all students and, in particular, students of color. To be sure, some programs and services have been more successful than others. However, this chapter has suggested that there are additional ways to think about how to equip students of color for collegiate success, and many of these alternatives involve activities provided to students even before they set foot on a college campus.

I have taken issue in this chapter with models that assume low-income, urban students of color must drop or reconfigure their cultures and identities of origin if they are to succeed in college. I have also pointed out that economic assistance is a necessary but insufficient ingredient for ensuring these students' college access. My argument thus has been posited within a cultural framework, noting that Bourdieu's concepts of cultural capital and habitus are helpful to consider in this regard. As a result, minority students from inner-city neighborhoods can be perceived as requiring embodied and objectified capital and, ultimately institutionalized capital, if they are to gain access to college. Further, programs such as the NAI can be viewed as helping to develop agency among their participating students and families so that the habitus of these groups does not become a deterministic structure that merely reproduces the social order.

It should also be noted that one additional concern I have with Bourdieu's work in general, and with the idea of cultural capital in particular, is that one might implicitly assume that those who lack cultural capital are in some way deficient in a manner akin to those who proffer the "culture-of-poverty" viewpoint. From such a perspective, Tinto's model of student retention and attrition holds sway: if minority students are to succeed in education, they need to replace their existing culture with one that is based on mainstream notions. I do not subscribe to that view, however.

The NAI's success is framed not merely by a concern for generating cultural capital but also by its attention to issues of cultural integrity. The low-income and urban minority students whom it serves are viewed not as deficient but as exceptional. Minority youth are not "the problem." As McLaughlin (1993) has noted, programs that assume this to be the case "too often reinforce [these] youths' view that something is wrong with them, that they are somehow deficient" (p. 59). Instead, the high-achieving adolescents who participate in the NAI are viewed by program staff as persons of value. Their families and neighborhoods are neither ignored nor avoided. The NAI model maintains that the route to equipping students with the necessary skills to succeed in educational systems is through the affirmation of students' local contexts and identities. Thus, by employing a concept of cultural integrity, the NAI equips these students with embodied and objectified capital.

Obviously, given the above-average college-going rates of NAI graduates, the program is successful not only in retaining students in high school but also in enabling them to get into college. Again, however, the NAI does more than enable low-income African American students from inner-city Los Angeles to get into college. Its graduates' ability to succeed in college is not merely the result of their comprehension of this-or-that mathematical formula or their understanding of how to interpret a particular literary text. Rather, these students arrive on college campuses with an enhanced awareness of their cultural identities that equips them with the sense that they *belong* there. Certainly, such a sense of identity and self-efficacy is manifested when an adolescent has the linguistic and mathematical abilities to do college-level work, yet it also derives from an identity framework that affirms and supports notions of the students' cultural background. In effect, this occurs when the idea of stereotype threat is replaced with a structure of support that assumes that students have or can gain the requisite skills to be admitted to and thrive in college.

In a sense, then, what I have suggested in this chapter is an expanded notion of what Tinto has called academic and social integration. However, rather than demand that students of color attending mainstream institutions of higher education undergo initiation rites that inevitably lead to their cultural suicide, a more protean cultural model of academic life should prevail. Such a model should contend that students of color on predominantly White campuses be able to affirm, rather than reject, who they are. Campuses that adopt this model will not be sites of assimilation but, instead, sites of contestation and multiple interpretations. Individuals on these campuses will not struggle over the presently static model of culture but over more fluid and dynamic notions. In such settings, not only will students of color have a greater likelihood of gaining access to institutionalized capital, but the campuses themselves will become more democratic spheres of educational opportunity.

References

Bourdieu, P. (1977). *Outline of a theory of practice* (R. Nice, Trans.). Cambridge, UK: Cambridge University Press.

Bourdieu, P. (1986). The forms of capital. In J. G. Richardson (Ed.), *Handbook of theory and research for the sociology of education* (pp. 241–258). New York: Greenwood.

Braxton, J. M., Sullivan, A. V., & Johnson, R. M. (1997). Appraising Tinto's theory of college student departure. In J. C. Smart (Ed.), *Higher education: Handbook of theory and research* (Vol. XII, pp. 231–288). New York: Agathon.

Carnegie Commission on Higher Education. (1970). *A chance to learn: An action agenda for equal opportunity in higher education; A special report and recommendations.* New York: McGraw-Hill.

Colvin, R. L., & Sahagun, L. (1998, August 19). Number of dropouts declining, state says: College enrollments rise, but officials admit that improvement is slight. *Los Angeles Times*, pp. B2–B5.

Deyhle, D. (1995). Navajo youth and Anglo racism: Cultural integrity and resistance. *Harvard Educational Review, 65*(3), 403–444.

Durkheim, E. (1951). *Suicide* (J. A. Spaulding, Trans.). Glencoe, IL: Free Press.

Gladieux, L. E., & Swail, W. S. (1998). Financial aid is not enough: Improving the odds of college success. *The College Board Review, 185*, 11–21.

Horn, L., & Chen, X. (1998). *Toward resiliency: At-risk students who make it to college.* Washington, DC: U.S. Department of Education.

Hossler, D., Braxton, J., & Coopersmith, G. (1989). Understanding student college choice. In J. C. Smart (Ed.), *Higher education: Handbook of theory and research* (Vol. V, pp. 231–288). New York: Agathon.

McDermott, R., & Varenne, H. (1995). Culture as disability. *Anthropology & Education Quarterly, 26*(3), 324–348.

McDonough, P. (1997). *Choosing colleges: How social class and schools structure opportunity.* Albany: State University of New York Press.

McLaughlin, M. W. (1993). Embedded identities: Enabling balance in urban contexts. In S. B. Heath & M. W. McLaughlin (Eds.), *Identity and inner-city youth* (pp. 36–68). New York: Teachers College Press.

McPherson, M., & Shapiro, M. (1998). *The student aid game.* Princeton, NJ: Princeton University Press.

Mehan, H., Villanueva, I., Hubbard, L., & Lintz, A. (1996). *Constructing school success: The consequences of untracking low-achieving students.* New York: Cambridge University Press.

O'Connor, C. (1997). Dispositions toward (collective) struggle and educational resilience in the inner city: A case analysis of six African-American high school students. *American Educational Research Journal, 34*(4), 593–629.

Perna, L. W., & Swail, W. S. (1998). *Early intervention programs: How effective are they at increasing access to college?* Paper presented at the annual meeting of the Association for the Study of Higher Education, Miami, FL.

Spindler, G., & Spindler, L. (1989). There are no dropouts among the Arunta and Hutterites. In H. T. Trueba, G. Spindler, & L. Spindler (Eds.), *What do anthropologists have to say about dropouts?* (pp. 7–15). New York: Falmer.

Steele, C. M. (1997). A threat in the air: How stereotypes shape intellectual identity and performance. *American Psychologist, 52*(6), 613–629.

St. John, E. (1990). Price response in enrollment decisions: An analysis of the high school and beyond sophomore cohort. *Research in Higher Education, 31,* 161–176.

Tierney, W. G. (1992). An anthropological analysis of student participation in college. *Journal of Higher Education, 63*(6), 603–618.

Tierney, W. G. (1996). Affirmative action in California: Looking back, looking forward in public academe. *Journal of Negro Education, 65*(2), 122–132.

Tierney, W. G. (1997). The parameters of affirmative action: Equity and excellence in the academy. *Review of Educational Research, 67*(2), 165–196.

Tierney, W. G. (2000). Power, identity, and the dilemma of college student departure. In J. M. Braxton (Ed.), *Rethinking the departure puzzle: New theory and research on college student retention* (pp. 259–283). Nashville, TN: Vanderbilt University Press.

Tierney, W. G., & Jun, A. (2001). A university helps prepare low-income youth for college: Tracking school success. *Journal of Higher Education, 72*(2), 205–225.

Tinto, V. (1987). *Leaving college: Rethinking the causes and cures of student attrition.* Chicago: University of Chicago Press.

Van Gennep, A. (1960). *The rites of passage* (M. Vizedon & G. Caffee, Trans.). Chicago: University of Chicago Press.

Varenne, H., & McDermott, R. (1998). *Successful failure: The school America builds.* Boulder, CO: Westview.

Wright, B., & Tierney, W. G. (1991). American Indians in higher education: A history of cultural conflict. *Change, 23*(2), 11–18.

8

A CULTURAL PERSPECTIVE ON COMMUNICATION AND GOVERNANCE

"I find it ironic," said one professor, "that you can be a faculty member here and never hear from the senate. You would think there would be some correspondence, or the representative from your school would come to faculty meetings to provide some indication of what the senate is doing." The professor's observation is on target. The role of communication in the governance of academic organizations is frequently underestimated or, more likely, ignored. Instead, studies of governance generally involve structural or role-related analysis. Some scholars discuss the strengths and weaknesses of an academic senate or assembly, for example, and consider its size, composition, and functions in relation to its effectiveness. Others evaluate the relative power of a particular position within a governing body, such as the presidency, or the role of mid-level functionaries, such as department chairs or deans.

In this chapter we consider the role of communication in academic governance. We suggest that, to become more effective in governance, faculty should focus on communicative strategies in addition to structural reforms. All too often, however, when faculty believe their power is diminished or their voice is limited, they argue solely for structural changes to one or another academic body. Although we do not dispute that on some campuses an overhaul of a decision-making body such as an academic senate is useful,

This chapter originally appeared as Tierney, W. G., & Minor, J. T. (2004). A cultural perspective on communication and governance. In W. G. Tierney & V. M. Lechuga (Eds.), Shared governance in higher education. *New Directions for Higher Education, 127*, 85–94. San Francisco: Jossey-Bass.

we assert that it is necessary to consider the interpretive potential of organizational life. Colleges and universities are not simply the sum of the structural units that produce and disseminate knowledge within them; they are also places where symbolic and abstract cultural meanings are created. From an interpretive perspective, these symbols and meanings are in part the by-product of the cultural processes that an organization's actors create in communicating with one another. It is these processes and communicative acts that we wish to consider here. We argue that the culture of the organization determines communication, and that communication helps constitute governance.

Our two reference points for analysis are a survey of shared governance that included 763 institutions and a group of eight case studies of 4-year colleges and universities. We begin with an overview of the communicative frameworks of governance and then discuss three central aspects of communication: situated meaning, speech and literacy events, and symbols and ceremonies. The goals of the chapter are to highlight the ways in which people communicate with one another and to suggest that communication is a key component of successful shared governance.

Governance by Conversation

Lewis B. Mayhew (1974) wrote the following about the governance structure of the modern university: "In one sense the governance of [the] university is governance by conversation. Many of the seemingly critical matters, such as the form of the curriculum or even the size of the budget . . . are the subject of thousands of hours of consultation and conversation before a final decision is ratified" (p. 58). Indeed, it would be impossible to chart how decisions are made in a traditional college or university. Unlike in a business, where an organizational map can at least approximate the path of decision making, at a college or university, ideas rarely follow a specific route to their implementation. When one looks, for example, at the issues before faculty senates at different colleges and universities, one finds that issues vary among institutions and even within institutions from one year to the next. Further, at some institutions senates are key faculty-governing bodies, while at others they are inconsequential or nonexistent (Tierney & Minor, 2003). In a universe of 4,000 postsecondary institutions, one certainly can expect a degree of variability among senates. In some senates, for example, all faculty are included, while in others, faculty are represented by academic unit or popular vote. In some cases executive committees are chosen by the entire faculty, in others they are selected by the senate itself. Some senate presidents are elected faculty members, others are the president or academic vice president of the institution.

Structurally, then, one cannot anticipate that a specific governing body will deal with particular issues regardless of institutional type or context. Among institutions, however, the delineation of formal faculty voice is relatively clear. More than 75% of the respondents to the survey stated that faculty had substantial influence in determining undergraduate curriculum, standards for promotion and tenure, and standards for the evaluation of teaching. There was equal agreement among participants that faculty had relatively little formal influence in setting budget priorities or evaluating the president and provost. Perceptual indicators, however, show divergent views. For example, when asked about the quality of communication among campus constituents in decision making, 88% of academic vice presidents agreed that it was good, or sufficient to make progress, compared to just 66% of faculty who agreed.

Although faculty claimed to have little formal influence in certain types of decisions, they reported having considerable informal influence. Both formal and informal influence were evident in many different types of governance structures. Although more than 85% of all four-year institutions have some form of a faculty governing body, most individuals reported academic departments, standing faculty committees, and ad hoc committees as substantial venues for participation. One faculty member of 26 years responded: "Like many other institutions, we make decisions based on the outcomes of multiple formal and informal conversations."

One commonsense observation of this process is that, among organizations, structures vary a great deal. Regardless of which venues are employed for deliberations by faculty, decisions are reached through communicative processes that take place within and outside those structures. Our point here is more than simply to assert that one group communicates by formal pathways and another by informal means. We suggest that the manner in which groups communicate with one another highlights underlying cultural beliefs within the organization. In turn, the way in which a college's or university's actors create the culture of the organization determines a host of critical issues pertaining to the faculty's role in governance.

Accordingly, if it is determined that faculty voice should be increased or taken more seriously in the governance of an institution, then an appropriate strategy for achieving this goal would be to consider the communicative processes employed within the organization. One fruitful way to analyze organizational communication is to consider how meaning is situated, what constitutes speech and literacy events, and how communicative symbols and ceremonies are used and by whom. As will become clear, each of these ideas frames an understanding of how communication functions as a cultural process within an organization.

Situated Meaning

Linguists have defined situated meaning as an understanding of the specific context that is transformed and negotiated by rules of speaking, which reflect the actors' relationships to, and attitudes toward, one another and the issues under consideration (Hymes, 1974). Although rules exist in any institution, in an academic organization populated by highly verbal participants who frequently seek to understand underlying structures, they are particularly important. Thus, we need to come to terms not only with the contexts in which communication takes place, such as a faculty senate, and the actors involved in the specific structure, such as a senate president, but also with the wider sociopolitical structures in which the communicative processes are embedded.

Investigations of shared governance need to move away from purely structural or outcome-related analysis. Looking only to a senate, for example, to define the types of issues that will be addressed, ignores the ways in which messages are created by the organization's culture. Similarly, to argue simply that the faculty's power and authority can be gauged by decisions made in a senate or committee is to disregard the idea that communication transcends decisions and outcomes. No one has ever plausibly advanced the argument that any one system of shared governance is better than the rest, nor has anyone demonstrated that a particular system necessitates that faculty bodies formally vote on all issues that come before it.

To consider the situated meaning of communication, one must identify who is and who is not involved in governance, the venues where governance takes place, and the formal and informal means used to communicate. Such an approach has broad implications for the study and analysis of shared governance. Studies of academic decision making frequently describe faculty governance in either/or terms: either an institution has an effective faculty senate, or its system of faculty governance is a sham. Rather than assume that everyone must participate in faculty governance for it to be effective, we posit that the history, culture, and present contexts of an institution frame governance in important ways. What Clark (1970) defined as a "distinctive college" (p. 234), for example, might have active faculty involvement on myriad topics, whereas a research university might seek faculty engagement in only a handful of issues. A campus with collective bargaining is likely to communicate in ways quite different from a campus without such an agreement. The point of our analysis is not to determine the best structure of governance for all institutions, or to imply that certain roles must have more authority. Instead, we seek to explore how an organization's participants make meaning based on the confines of the institutional context.

Literacy and Speech Events

A literacy event takes place when a piece of writing plays an integral role in shaping meaning and interactions among participants. Speech events are oral in nature and surround literacy events. As Heath (1982) has noted, "Speech events may describe, repeat, reinforce, expand, frame or contradict written materials, and participants must learn whether the oral or written mode takes precedence in literacy events" (p. 93). Obviously, in an academic community, a wealth of literacy events takes place, and speech events circumscribe organizational decisions. With the advent of websites and the Internet, literacy events have increased dramatically, just as conference calls and voice-activated referencing have led to an increase in speech events. A student newspaper, a faculty forum, a university newspaper, a senate Web page, and the minutes and agenda for meetings are examples of literacy events. Each piece of writing pertains to some aspect of decision making. It informs various constituencies about decisions to be made or actions taken. Writing may be used to explain actions, to argue for or against a particular idea, or to inform debate. Written materials help shape an argument.

Speech events generally take place with participants face-to-face and involve literacy events. Individuals may refer to a text or extrapolate from it, confer individually or as a group, and so on. They might speak formally or informally. An example of a formal speech act that involves a literacy event would be the approval of meeting minutes with changes to the written text suggested orally by a committee member. An example of an informal speech event that involves literacy events could be the gossip or conversation that occurs before or after a meeting about a memo that has been sent or received.

Speech and literacy events, then, are oral and written messages communicated to an organization's constituencies. Such messages have distinct temporal frames. They can be divided into four types: preparational, presentational, preservational, and promotional. Each event has not only a distinct time frame but also a purpose within that time frame. For example, before making necessary changes to the institution, a group may use a Web page to develop white papers that discuss why the faculty need to revamp general education. Or, perhaps, when a presentation is being prepared for a curricular affairs committee, ideas for specific changes may be debated among faculty. Once decisions of any type are made, a faculty handbook may be amended to create institutional memory of the revision. Finally, one may use a literacy event to promote and communicate decisions that have been made by the governing body. Such analysis enables us to understand how members make use of particular documents and materials within governance.

When analyzing literacy and speech events, the roles of central and peripheral actors need to be considered. This information is particularly important with regard to shared governance because speech events occur between speakers and listeners. Similarly, a literacy event is an interaction over a text that someone has written and someone else reads. Consider, for example, perhaps the most serious action an academic community might contemplate: the removal of an individual faculty member's tenure. Numerous literacy events come into play—the faculty handbook, the institution's grievance policy, and all documents pertaining directly to the case. The dismissal proceedings and the hearings of the case are examples of speech events. In analyzing these speech events, it is necessary to consider carefully who instigates the proceedings and who is involved in the hearings. These events are not disembodied scripts devoid of speakers, listeners, authors, and readers. If a faculty committee brings forth a cause for dismissal, the meaning of the scripts may well differ from those if the administration were to do the same. Literacy and speech events inevitably are defined by the situated meaning infused by an organization's actors, history, and culture.

In one light, the kind of analysis described here does little more than state the obvious: minutes are taken at senate meetings, and individuals make oral changes to written documents that are then preserved. A university president's memo to the faculty about general education carries different meanings than an assistant professor's message on a faculty listserv. In this chapter, however, we argue a different point. Shared governance is more than a functional analysis of whether faculty members vote on a particular issue or whether a certain clause exists in the faculty handbook to guarantee protections. Shared governance is a cultural undertaking that reinscribes what the academic community believes about itself. These beliefs help define the speakers, listeners, authors, and readers of speech and literacy events. Just as one needs to analyze the specific protections guaranteed to faculty in a contract to ensure that academic freedom is preserved, a college or university must attend to the cultural interpretations given to communication to achieve effective governance. To ignore these interpretations permits an incomplete understanding of academic governance.

Communicative Symbols and Ceremonies

Manifest messages of governance and the latent and symbolic cultural meanings of an institution also merit attention. As Feldman and March observed, "Organizational structures and processes often have symbolic importance to participants" (cited in Birnbaum, 1989, p. 428). The composition of faculty senates and university committees, the absence or presence of the president at a meeting, and the participation or absence of the provost in promotion and tenure meetings all send messages to the community about governance. These messages are highly unstable and vary from campus to campus. They change over time and exemplify the latent and shifting cultural meanings created within academic communities.

Active faculty participation in governance might indicate to the academic world that a college or university is in the postsecondary mainstream. A for-profit college that relies entirely on part-time faculty who utilize distance learning may seek to legitimize itself by creating a virtual academic senate to prove that it is not so different from traditional institutions. The addition of a promotion and tenure committee that includes requirements about the need to do research at an institution that has no history of doing research may signify that the university aims to rise in the traditional academic hierarchy. Statements about academic freedom that refer to the American Association of University Professors (1966) place an institution in line with mainstream ideas about the topic. Conversely, a statement that stipulates a narrow interpretation of academic freedom made by a representative of a religious institution may be a purposeful symbolic message that the college or university has made a conscious decision to distance itself from the mainstream.

It is important to recognize that symbols and ceremonies, as interpretive acts, rarely have a singular meaning. A president's absence from senate meetings may indicate that the president's schedule is too full, but senators may interpret this absence as an affront to shared governance. The faculty's extended deliberations over a move to dismiss a colleague accused of terrorist acts may appear to external constituencies as foot-dragging, whereas the faculty may perceive it to be evidence of their devotion to due process and academic freedom. A faculty committee that votes to move from an all-faculty assembly to a smaller group of elected representatives may be motivated by trying to increase faculty voice. However, others might see the change as an attempt to stifle faculty voice. Attending to the symbolic side of academic life is necessary to improve governance. Therefore, those who seek to rethink how governance functions at their institution need to take into account the specific symbolic and cultural meanings that infuse an organization's structures.

Perceptions of governance on a campus are determined in part by the ceremonies and culture that exist within those organizational structures. Ceremonies are important sites for the analysis of the values of an academic community. At some institutions, for example, during convocation, a faculty member, perhaps the president of the senate, will lead the procession of faculty, administrators, and graduates in the ceremony. The message of this action is that the faculty "lead" the institution. Similarly, when faculty recommend candidates for an honorary doctorate to a board of trustees, they simultaneously highlight their ceremonial and "real" roles in shared governance. Ceremonies provide individuals with a sense of membership and integration in an organization. They convey to faculty that they are not simply members of a guild, but, rather, that they play a central role in determining the institution's well-being and future. An organization deprived of ceremonies that celebrate or dramatize organizational values is one in which little explicit attention is paid to the cultural aspects of academic life. A de-ritualized organization is one bereft of meaning. In such cases, the actors have assumed that the institution is a collection of instrumentalities in which decisions are made through chains of command. While one cannot dispute the benefits of effective and efficient procedures for an institution, if one ignores the cultural aspects of organizational life, one runs the risk of overlooking the invisible bonds of communal affiliation that tie the members of the professorate to their institutions and to one another.

Improving Communication and Governance

For those who subscribe to a cultural view of the academic world and are concerned about enhancing faculty involvement in governance, at least two central suggestions logically follow the arguments raised here.

Focus on Communicative Pathways

David Leslie (1996) has argued cogently that "change in colleges and universities comes when it happens in the trenches; what faculty and students do is what the institution becomes. It does not happen because a committee or a president asserts a new idea" (p. 110). Unfortunately, there is often a temptation to revert to old-fashioned notions of power, so "where the buck stops" indicates who has the final authority. If the buck does not pass by the faculty or if individuals believe that the buck actually stops at the faculty's doorstep, then governance does not appear to be shared. From a cultural perspective, however, governance needs to be more than a basic check of who gets to vote and who is denied the opportunity to do so.

Shared governance does not result solely from the formal allocation of spheres of responsibility and authority (Trow, 1990). Instead, informal arrangements and processes should be interpreted by the academic collective with regard to the relative influence of different academic bodies and the significance of different decisions. It is important to recognize that faculty involvement in governance occurs on many levels and in many forums. Simply because faculty do not vote on a preponderance of issues does not mean that shared governance is not functioning. Meaningful involvement is achieved when multiple constituencies are able to communicate with one another across multiple venues.

Colleges and universities exist in "loosely coupled" environments (Weick, 1976, p. 3). A mistaken tendency among those attempting to improve faculty governance is to try to tighten this loose coupling. Far too often individuals assume that, for meaningful engagement to occur, all decisions must be processed through a governance structure such as a senate. Such a mind-set creates the potential for faculty governance to deal with just a few issues over the course of a year. Instead, those involved would be better advised to accept that institutions exist in decentralized organizations and that the faculty's engagement with an issue may be sporadic. Effective governance, then, is defined not so much by the presence of an efficient structure or the number of votes the faculty concludes in a year. Effective governance pertains more to the understanding and management of meaning such that the core values of the faculty and of the institution are not merely preserved, but advanced.

Accept the Potency of Speech and Literacy Events

Those who understand the symbolic functions of speech and literacy events within an organization are more likely to use these communicative vehicles than are those who ignore them. At a time when faculty have numerous communicative outlets at their disposal, it is imperative that they use them in a systematic fashion. As analysis of typical speech and literacy events at colleges or universities demonstrates, too often it appears as if the administration owns the airwaves. The alumni office puts out the university magazine. The president's office issues quarterly newsletters. The provost's office publishes a weekly news magazine and has periodic e-updates to advertise a particular idea. The provost currently is engaged in writing a strategic plan and has sent drafts to the entire faculty asking for feedback. The office of information services reports to the vice president for administration and manages the university's website. The deans send out weekly bulletins on listservs for their individual schools and a biannual update to donors, alumni, students, and faculty regarding the state of the school.

Meanwhile, the faculty senate tries to publish one or two newsletters a year that arrive three months late. Its website is seldom updated, so one is never really sure what topics are being addressed. The faculty have created a campus-wide listserv, but after a heated debate about whether faculty messages should be edited or simply published, only two kinds of messages have appeared: occasional announcements about sublets from faculty who are about to depart on sabbatical, and messages from three professors who do not hesitate to use the listserv to expound on their most recent complaint. As a result, a third of the faculty also has removed itself from the listserv.

Such a portrait may seem like a caricature of academic life, but unfortunately, this scenario often closely reflects the reality of the situation. Some will respond that the administration naturally does a better job of communicating with the academic community, as they have both resources and time at their disposal. At the same time, some leaders are better at symbolic management than others. Faculty who are concerned about governance need to consider ways to communicate a message in a timely, concerted, and systematic manner. Yet, in an era when technology has increased our capability to communicate, faculty communication with one another and with university administration seems to have decreased. Administrators have mastered ways to get their message out. In contrast, faculty often do not seem to recognize the importance of communication, which returns us to the central precept of this chapter.

Communication is not a cure-all for the current woes that confront those involved in shared governance, but a concern for organizational reform must be balanced with an awareness of the communicative codes within the workplace. Academic organizations are rich in cultural meanings. Intellectual work, in part, involves the understanding, decoding, and manipulation of symbolic messages. If faculty follow such methods in their intellectual endeavors, they can use a similar, critical approach in their efforts to improve shared governance within their academic communities.

References

American Association of University Professors. (1966). *Statement on government of colleges and universities.* Washington, DC: Author. Retrieved May 4, 2008, from http://www.aaup.org/

Birnbaum, R. (1989). The latent organizational functions of the academic senate: Why senates do not work but will not go away. *The Journal of Higher Education, 60*(4), 423–443.

Clark, B. (1970). *The distinctive college: Antioch, Reed, and Swarthmore.* Chicago: Aldine.

Heath, S. (1982). Protean shapes in literacy events. In D. Tannen (Ed.), *Spoken and written language* (pp. 91–117). Norwood, NJ: Ablex.

Hymes, D. (1974). Ways of speaking. In R. Bauman and J. Sherzer (Eds.), *Explorations in the ethnography of speaking* (pp. 433–452). Cambridge, UK: Cambridge University Press.

Leslie, D. (1996). Strategic governance: The wrong questions? *Review of Higher Education, 20*(1), 101–112.

Mayhew, L. B. (1974). *Administration and governance of the university.* Unpublished manuscript.

Tierney, W. G., & Minor, J. T. (2003). *Challenges for governance: A national report.* Los Angeles: Center for Higher Education Policy Analysis, University of Southern California.

Trow, M. (1990). The academic senate as a school for university leadership. *Liberal Education, 76*(1), 23–27.

Weick, K. E. (1976). Educational organizations as loosely coupled systems. *Administrative Science Quarterly, 21*(1), 1–19.

PART THREE

THE ROAD AHEAD

9

A CULTURAL ANALYSIS OF SHARED GOVERNANCE

The Challenges Ahead

F or over a century the concept of shared governance has held a prominent place in the culture and mythology of academic organizations.
Indeed, when one speaks of the structure of colleges and universities,
an inescapable discussion revolves around participative governance. For
some, shared governance is a central totem of the academy; if academe did
not have shared governance, then one's conception of a college or university
inevitably would change. For others, shared governance is the root cause of
many of academe's problems; if administrators were able to eliminate or
overhaul academe's governance structures, then postsecondary institutions
might become more strategic and efficient. In doing so, administrators
would be better able to deal with the myriad problems that currently exist
for colleges and universities. At least three issues arise with regard to these
differing perceptions of shared governance.

First, the tenor of the literature on shared governance often reads like
either a call to arms or a funeral oration. Whether one wants to reinvigorate
shared governance or destroy it, the discourse is frequently overheated and
bombastic. "The classic strategy," wrote Joanna Vecchiarelli Scott (1996) in
describing recent changes, "is what might be termed a stealth attack on governance launched under cover of summer vacations" (p. 724). In another
article, Scott (1997) portrayed the takeover of governance as a crime scene

This chapter originally appeared as Tierney, W. G. (2004). A cultural analysis of shared governance: The
challenges ahead. *Higher Education: Handbook of Theory and Research* (Vol. 19, pp. 85–132). Norwell, MA:
Kluwer Academic.

(p. 28). Victor Baldridge (1982) wrote, "We hear much weeping about the loss of shared governance" (p. 13). Faculty senates are "dysfunctional" (Leatherman, 1998, p. A8) to others, and, adopting a medical metaphor, critics suggest that the patient (the institution) is dying and in need of a transplant; the need for governance reform is "urgent" (Association of Governing Boards of Universities and Colleges [AGB], 1996).

Second, although there is a great deal of hand-wringing about shared governance, the vast majority of the literature is anecdotal and atheoretical. When thoughtful studies of governance have been done, they are usually at the state level and have less to do with governance per se than with ways to enhance statewide coordination (Ewell, 1985, 1990; McGuinness, 1994; Richardson, Bracco, Callan, & Finney, 1999). As Dill and Helm (1988) have noted, there is very limited contemporary research on governance structures (p. 327). Instead, scholars have tended to focus on leadership, defined as the college presidency (e.g., Birnbaum, 1988) or on decision making (e.g., Leslie & Fretwell, 1996; Schuster, Smith, Corak, & Yamada, 1994). The lack of theoretical frameworks denies us the ability to diagnose governance from a particular vantage point, which, in turn, forces suggestions for improvement to be based on intuition rather than a logically nuanced framework.

Third, shared governance is a term that is casually used with implicit meanings and little intellectual rigor. Indeed, more often than not, authors who use the concept neither build on previous definitions nor bring into question what has been incorporated into, and excluded from, the term. Shared governance is a concept that has assumed an honorific stature in most academic writing. Even those critics who wish to dramatically change governance processes quite frequently cling to the desire to call those changes a permutation of shared governance. Thus, for some individuals, shared governance is ahistorical and simply means what one desires it to mean. For others, shared governance is a static concept that was enshrined by the American Association of University Professors (AAUP) in 1967. On the one side, then, are fundamentalists who subscribe to a literal, unchanging interpretation of the term. On the other side are scholars who are the equivalent of postmodern deconstructionists and who believe the term changes based on current contexts.

My purpose here is to shed light on these various meanings of shared governance, and to explicate the underlying premises, problems, and challenges. I take issue with many previous definitions of shared governance, not for what they say, but for what they leave out. As I will elaborate, governance in any organization is a process devised to achieve particular outcomes. If the problems that academe currently faces are to be resolved, one needs to question the processes used to resolve these problems. One also needs to be certain of the core values that circumscribe an organization. Values are not processes; they are beliefs and goals that lead to outcomes. Processes, however, are symbolic of the organization's culture. They are emblematic of what the organization's participants believe is important. As symbols, processes such as shared governance are embedded in sociocultural contexts that undergo constant reinterpretation because of the entrance of new participants who bring new meanings to the organization's culture. And yet, these symbols underscore the values of the organization.

The literature is replete with examples of how colleges and universities differ from standard organizations. A goal of a large company, for example, will be based on profit, whereas the same cannot be said about a traditional college. A belief that customer satisfaction is a key value may be central in a company such as Wal-Mart, but in a university, use of the term "customer" may be anathema. I will suggest that there are values that can be delineated for a college or university, and in doing so, one can then suggest the parameters of shared governance. I will argue that the core values of academe enable an institution's participants to maintain an identity, and that these values are neither static nor illusory. In effect, I will challenge the thinking that a statement made a generation ago is not open to reinterpretation, but I also will question that such a reinterpretation is open to any definition an author wishes to provide. I will argue that shared governance as a symbolic process underscores fundamental values of the academy. Rather than conflate a process—shared governance—as a static structure, we need to be cognizant of the values embedded in the idea of governance and ensure that such values remain constant as structures and processes adapt to the times.

I will advance this argument in three parts. I first discuss previous definitions of shared governance and point out how the definitions do not so much contradict one another as they take up entirely *different* issues. I then consider the frames of reference that have been employed to analyze and define shared governance. I conclude with a discussion of the problems and concerns that have been elaborated with regard to shared governance, offer possible ways to ameliorate those problems, sketch the lineaments of what I will define as a cultural definition of shared governance, and, finally, offer suggestions about areas in need of research. One note of caution: I will use the organization as the unit of analysis, and I call upon the literature on shared governance that pertains to four-year colleges and universities. As I discuss at the conclusion, I entirely concur that similar explications of shared governance need to occur with regard to community colleges, state systems, and the burgeoning number of for-profit institutions. At the same time, the vast majority of literature on shared governance deals with four-year institutions; my first project is to consider the literature that exists in order to develop scaffolding for a cultural analysis of shared governance and a sense of promising research areas.

Defining Shared Governance

The point of departure for most discussions about shared governance is the statement written and endorsed by the AAUP in 1967 and "commended" by the American Council on Education (ACE) and the Association of Governing Boards of Universities and Colleges (AGB). The authors of the document recognized that a variety and complexity of tasks performed by institutions of higher education produced an "inescapable interdependence" (AAUP, 2001, p. 218). The argument was put forth that, although different decisions might be made by one or another constituency, some decisions necessitated "the initiating capacity and decision making participation of all the institutional components" (p. 218). The document relied extensively on a definition of governance that pertained to who shared in decision making.

In 1998 AGB came forward with its own endorsement of a definition of institutional governance. The authors of the AGB report studiously avoided using the term "shared governance." AGB began by pointing out that much had changed since the 1967 AAUP statement. The authors opined that reduced fiscal resources, greater demands of accountability, competition from new providers, and a host of related issues necessitated a new statement on internal governance. The assumptions that drove the text were that "internal governance arrangements have become so cumbersome that timely decisions are difficult to make, and small factions often are able to impede the decision making process" (AGB, 1998, p. 5). The result, claimed AGB, was that even if decisions were reached on a particular issue, because of the search for consensus, the least-objectionable option was frequently chosen.

Although the AAUP and AGB statements are not diametrically opposed to one another, there are significant differences between them. The AGB report portrayed a more hierarchical organization in which a board had ultimate authority to make decisions and the faculty were one of many stakeholders. The AAUP statement assumed a flatter organizational structure in which faculty, administrators, and the board discussed issues with one another in a more collegial process. The AGB statement also tended to rely more on a market-driven mission for academe in which the board decided its strategic plan in consultation with the president, and the AAUP authors opted for a jointly formulated strategic plan that focused on traditional conceptions of the university.

In a carefully nuanced analysis, Neil Hamilton (1999) compared the two statements and concluded that they "share much more common ground than the language of each suggests" (p. 26). He pointed out that the AAUP always had agreed that ultimate responsibility for the determination of the mission lay with the board, and that the AGB report still ceded to the faculty greater say with regard to curricular decisions and faculty appointments. Hamilton also cautioned the various academic communities not to devolve into an "us versus them" mentality. He encouraged all groups to accept the responsibility of the public trust for colleges and universities and defined that trust as the inextricable connections of "mission, academic freedom, and shared governance" (p. 26).

Hamilton touched on a helpful point that is often overlooked: what is the purpose of governance in general, and shared governance in particular? Often authors speak of shared governance as an end, rather than a process. For Hamilton, the mission of higher education is the creation and dissemination of knowledge. The role of shared governance is to help achieve those purposes. The search to cut costs and to be effective and efficient are important principles, Hamilton argued, but they are not the mission. And yet, even Hamilton conflated shared governance with "mission" and "academic freedom" as if shared governance were an end in itself, or the only possible structure that would enable an institution's participants to achieve its mission.

Presumably, without shared governance, academe would not be academe. One needs to make a careful distinction between the values of an organization and the symbols that express those values. If one assumes that the symbol, the artifact, is the actual value, then one has little ability to create change. Consider, for example, the manner in which the Catholic Church conducts Mass. A half-century ago the altar was turned away from the congregants and the priest spoke in Latin. Those symbols expressed values of the Church; when the Church decided to turn the altar around and have the priests speak in the local dialect, the values of the Church did not change, but the symbolic processes did. To be sure, the changes caused consternation among more than a few individuals, but the Church's purpose in doing so was to try to enrich its long-standing values with symbolic meaning for parishioners of the 20th century.

Symbolic change frequently causes anger and resentment because many consider the symbol to have substantive meaning and value. Consider the current debate about whether women can be priests or if priests can marry. The argument revolves around the meaning of the symbolic change. Celibacy among men is merely an outmoded symbol to some congregants, and to others the symbol has actual meaning and purpose. The assumption is that when one changes the symbol, a value of the organization changes as well; the challenge for those who drive change is to assure the various participants that the core values of the organization remain. Thus, the change of a symbolic process is most often not easy, but one also ought not to assume that symbols are unchangeable.

Martin Trow (1998) disagreed somewhat with Hamilton on the purpose of governance. He offered two overarching principles: "These two principles are the maximization of the University's autonomy—its capacity to direct its own affairs; and second, the pursuit of preeminence" (p. 202). Although one might assume that Trow was speaking about academic freedom when he mentioned autonomy, he actually had a different value in mind. Autonomy referred to the removal of politics from academic decisions so that the university might be a meritocracy. The pursuit of preeminence also had less to do with fiscal stability than with academic quality. Shared governance, then, inoculated the university from political interference and enabled the faculty to pursue excellence. The framework for excellence was defined as a meritocracy, and an effective system of shared governance ensured that evaluation occurred by judging the merit of one's work. One should note that Trow's work focused primarily on public institutions, whereas the AGB and AAUP statements were intended for all institutions.

Henry Rosovsky (1990), former dean of the faculty at Harvard, offered a slightly different assessment. He noted that governance should improve the capacity for teaching and research (p. 276). Governance also pertained to power, argued Rosovsky: "Who is in charge; who makes decisions; who has a voice, and how loud is that voice?" (p. 261). Governance, to Rosovsky (2001), was the formal and informal arrangements of power and authority that enabled decisions to be carried out (p. 95). Cynthia Hardy (1990) also relied less on the philosophical purpose of governance and more on its function: "Governance is used to refer to the process of making academic decisions" (p. 393). Barbara Lee (1991) further defined the function of governance "as the way that issues affecting the entire institution, or one or more components thereof, are decided" (p. 41).

In part, these various interpretations of academic governance appear a bit like the proverbial blind man describing an elephant: the position of the author determines what the individual will write about and how he or she will describe the shared elephant. One might expect a professional organization concerned with faculty such as the AAUP to call for a greater commitment to shared decision making, and for an association composed of corporate businesspeople such as the AGB to be concerned with fiscal security. A former dean of the faculty at a private institution may well think of governance as an internally defined political exercise, whereas a professor in an elite public institution may be concerned with helping the institution move up in the rankings, increase its prestige, and remain insulated from external interference. These disparate definitions frequently conflict and collide with one another. One way to highlight the differences among the various definitions is to consider how to evaluate whether an institution has an effective governance structure based on the interpretations that have been outlined.

From an AAUP perspective, "The ideal governance model is one in which collaboration among the various governance components is the rule" (Ramo, 1998, p. 6). In this light the process of governance is what matters. Outcomes are irrelevant. One might, for example, see the institution slide into fiscal jeopardy, but claim that as long as the various constituencies collaborate, there is good governance. To be fair, the implicit assumption is that shared governance ensures "good" outcomes—but those outcomes have neither been explicated nor tested. The AGB will obviously disagree that outcomes are irrelevant. It might argue that processes are less important than ensuring that the institution is fiscally secure. A concern for academic freedom or the improvement of teaching would be incidental—except as they pertain to the enhancement of the fiscal stability and health of the institution.

Rosovsky's approach would investigate how governance has helped or hindered teaching and learning, whereas Trow would hinge the assessment on academic excellence, which at a research university frequently has little to do with teaching. Presumably if teaching and learning were not improving, or if the institution were not rising in the ranks, then one could justifiably question why the governance structures were failing. The assumption, of course, is that governance enables (or impedes) quality. Teaching, research, and institutional quality do not occur irrespective of the structures in which they are embedded. Simply stated: governance matters. Thus, from Hardy's (1990) and Lee's (1991) perspectives one will study the processes of governance to determine how one might improve what takes place. What is missing from their definitions, however, is how one assesses "good" governance. If one looks at the functions of the various processes of shared governance, what indicators might one use to ensure that it is functioning effectively? Is an absence of conflict, for example, an indicator of good governance or a moribund campus? Is an organization that is fiscally stable an indicator of a strong-willed administrator or a viable governance structure?

Nevertheless, the assumption of all of these disparate definitions is that governance structures make a difference. Curiously, there is very little research to support such an assertion, but virtually everyone assumes that governance is the engine that drives reform. My concern is that, unless individuals and constituencies work from common understandings of shared governance, everyone will repeatedly be at odds with one another. Accordingly, in what follows I outline the frames of governance to develop more fully a sense of what an overarching definition of governance from a cultural perspective might be.

Frames of Reference

One might analyze academic governance from any number of frameworks. Here I consider the most common frames that authors have used.

A Historical Framework

As with any topic, an understanding of the roots of an issue lends insight into how a topic has changed over time. As I commented, such an observation is particularly germane in discussions about shared governance insofar as today's participants frequently speak of governance as if what exists on their campus is the way governance exists everywhere and for all time. A historical lens points out significant discrepancies as well as continuities. As I will elaborate here, today's critics often paint current boards of trustees as if they are a historical aberration because their membership represents the business world. However, businesspeople have dominated boards of trustees for more than a century. Similarly, those who seek to imbue faculty senates with more power often suggest that such structures have been historical focal points for power and authority, whereas most senates have come into existence in the last half-century. A historical analysis is helpful in enabling students of governance processes to gain a sense of how different constituencies and structures have changed over time.

John Beach (1985) observed, for example, that in the 12th and 13th centuries, the University of Bologna was thought to be composed of the students; the faculty were hired servants who either succeeded or were fired without recourse to appeal or renewal (p. 304). In Paris the opposite was the case. The faculty ran the institution, and students attended it to learn. In the Middle Ages the Church thought of universities as purveyors of ecclesiastical doctrine; academic freedom would have been thought of as heresy. The Church originally granted permission for a university to open; only later was the emperor or king also endowed with the power to grant a charter. Such a charter permitted a form of self-governance in which the medieval professoriate functioned at a distance from the church structure as well as the state.

If there is one vestige of historical import that has framed academic life in the 21st century, it is the movement toward the establishment of a corporation with a lay board. The result has been twofold. On the one hand, the university has been relatively removed from the vagaries of public life. True, campuses have long been buffeted by the winds of change in their surroundings. Nevertheless, whether one speaks of the Reformation or the McCarthy era, however much intrusion existed, such interference was less for universities than for nonacademic organizations that were wedded to the state. To be sure, during the reign of Henry VIII and his successors, as with today's tension in Catholic institutions, there have been conflict and demands from external agents, but over time such problems have worked out relatively well with regard to self-governance.

On the other hand, a lay board also removed the faculty from direct governance of the institution. Although over time some institutions have allowed a representative or two from the faculty to sit on the board, the faculty by and large have never been the legal overseers of the academic corporation. Even the AAUP has never called for a change in such an arrangement. The overall control of an American university lies in the "trust" of the board.

One also might point out that American higher education reflects a uniquely Western European mode of organization. Although the first postsecondary institutions in the Americas were in Mexico and Latin America and were of Spanish origin, colleges and universities in the United States derive their identity from the United Kingdom and Germany. The establishment of colleges and universities in the colonies followed a European model and extended what the respected historian Walter Metzger (1987) referred to as "laicization" (p. 13). That is, American institutions extended ever further the assumption that nonacademic/nonclerical individuals had formal authority over the governance of the institution.

The other change that has continued throughout the history of the United States is that of privatization. Few countries have such an elaborate structure of private institutions that derive their support from nongovernmental sources. The implications for governance, of course, are significant. As the Dartmouth College case established, the state has no formal control over the organization of a private institution other than the ability to grant the institution legal authority, as is done with any corporation. The board of a private college or university has no relationship to the state, and interference from the state is even further removed than at public institutions.

Over time, of course, those individuals who have represented the interests of a particular constituency on a board have changed. Over a century ago the clergy dominated boards in ways that simply do not occur today, and agricultural interests were better represented in the 19th century than in the 21st. Representatives from society such as magistrates and judges have been well represented on boards. Currently, individuals are frequently chosen not because they are able to offer a religious aura or judicious advice, but because they have accumulated wealth. Insofar as wealth resides more with businesspeople than with, for example, teachers or truck drivers, a particular strata of society is represented on boards, but as I will discuss, such participation has existed for a century.

Although one may not need to return to a study of the Middle Ages whenever one wishes to change a particular aspect of current governance procedures, an understanding of the various phases of governance over the past century is helpful insofar as distinct phases have come and gone. The development of the concept of shared governance can be traced to about 1960. At that time, John Corson (1960) defined governance in higher education as the authority to create rules and regulations concerning the governing of the academy and the relationships among various constituencies with the organization. Such an interpretation had its antecedents planted more firmly in the 20th century than throughout the ages. Dill and Helm (1988) have spoken of three periods of governance in the modern era: faculty *control*, democratic *participation*, and strategic *policy making* (p. 321).

Faculty *control* most closely resembles what the AAUP referred to in its statement on governance. The underlying assumption of the AAUP about postsecondary institutions in the United States from the early part of the 20th century until the 1960s was that the faculty controlled the institution. The college or university ran as a collegium, and the faculty as a whole determined the direction of the organization. At times, scholars such as Thorstein Veblen (1918/1957) or Upton Sinclair (1923) railed against the intrusive nature of corporate America, but by and large the sentiment that existed about universities and colleges was that the faculty had a considerable voice in the institution. The administrative structure often was meager, and those individuals who were presidents were likely to be seen as leaders of the faculty rather than members of a separate entity.

To be sure, part of the view of a college or university as a collegium in the early 20th century is a romanticized vision of the past. Robert Hutchins, Herman Wells, and John Hannah, to name but a few university presidents during this period, exerted control over their institutions in a manner unheard of today. At the same time, the faculty organized themselves as professions during the 20th century in ways that had not previously been done in the United States. If faculty had not become professionals in the first half of the 20th century, then the second period of governance most likely could not have taken place.

Democratic *participation* had its genesis in the late 1950s and 1960s. The rise of faculty assemblies and senates and collective bargaining took hold. One is always able to debate the cause of an innovation, but certainly the rapid growth of higher education, a considerable influx of new students and faculty into academe, and the social and cultural events that were occurring in society led to a desire for discussions about how to make academe more representative. As Dill and Helm (1988) noted,

> [P]articularly at the most prestigious colleges and universities where faculty controlled the governance process, the dominant coalition of faculty members and administrators was confronted by demands to democratize the governance process and to include students and other disaffected constituencies in traditional faculty senates. (p. 322)

The result was that structural changes took place that ostensibly allowed for greater participation in academic governance than had been possible previously.

The rise of new institutions and collective bargaining also led to new twists in governance patterns. Community colleges, and teachers colleges that became state colleges or universities, did not have the history of governance of more traditional institutions. Of consequence, administrative, legislative, and bureaucratic forms of control were established more easily in these new organizations. Collective bargaining arrangements frequently redefined who was to participate and who might be considered "faculty." Librarians, for example, increasingly were included in collective bargaining arrangements and thought of as faculty who had a right to participate in governance. Thus, throughout the 1960s and 1970s there was a rapid rise in the formalization of governance under new arrangements, even though the basic premises remained the same.

In the past 20 years, however, there has been a significant change in governance patterns. The experimentation in democratic forms of governance has most likely seen its heyday. The formalization of authority in a faculty senate or academic assembly also has branched out to other decision-making venues as *strategic policy making* has risen in importance. Again, one might attribute these changes to any number of factors. With few exceptions, for at least a generation, postsecondary institutions have faced fiscal shortfalls that have led to calls for greater managerial involvement. Boards of trustees have become increasingly populated with more activist businesspeople who have expected colleges and universities to more closely resemble businesses. The country itself has become less interested in broad patterns of democratic participation such that the kind of governance structures one experienced on many campuses in the 1960s would seem anachronisms today.

The result is that when faculty participate in governance, they do so in multiple venues such as ad hoc or joint committees with administrators. As Dill and Helm (1988) summarized, "The tenets of faculty control and democratic participation were articulated during a period of growth and general prosperity for American higher education. The current environment of scarcity and competition is thus strange to both governance perspectives" (p. 324). Their debatable assumption, of course, is that faculty control and democratic forms of governance are anathema to dealing with an array of problems that arise during periods of fiscal shortfall. More flamboyantly, and without any supporting data, Amacher and Meiners (2002) also concluded, "The notion that there is some sort of collective wisdom in the faculty that justifies democratic decision making about most spheres of university operation is nonsense" (p. 34). Such an assertion, although certainly dyspeptic, is important because it represents a particular point of view about the need for a radical rethinking of what one means by shared governance.

Thus, one frame of governance comes by way of competing historical perceptions. A second framework to which we now turn pertains to the contexts and structures of governance that have been investigated. Context concerns institutional type and structure of the unit of analysis under study.

Contexts and Structures as a Framework

It is a truism of research in higher education that the overwhelming number of investigations that have been done are about the kinds of institutions where the researchers reside (Tierney, 1999). That is, most scholars who do research on higher education work in research universities, and most research looks at various issues that pertain to research universities. The same point may be made about research on governance. As noted, there is very little empirical work on governance in community colleges. Although for-profit institutions are a relatively new phenomenon, they also are not being investigated in any systematic or comprehensive manner. State systems of higher education have a robust literature, but most of it looks at the organization of the system relative to the state and compares that organization to other states' (Richardson et al., 1999). There is virtually no research, for example, on the role of faculty, students, or community members on state boards.

Similarly and commonsensically, one also studies that which can be studied. Thus, very few works have investigated, in any rigorous manner, members of boards of trustees. The most extensive body of research derives from the research arm of the AGB. Chait, Holland, and Taylor (1991, 1996) also wrote two works on the role of boards of trustees in institutional governance, and William Bowen (1994) offered armchair advice about board effectiveness; but other than their studies, most research on governance has looked elsewhere. A small body of research also has looked at nonprofit boards (Chait & Taylor, 1989; Taylor, Chait, & Holland, 1996); such work has included a discussion of postsecondary boards. Gaining entrance to a board is frequently a hurdle that researchers cannot overcome, so even though boards are a critically important component of governance, they are also the least-studied structural configuration in academe. When boards are studied, the manner of investigation is most often not through interview or case study, but through document analysis.

Hubert Beck, for example, studied the economic and social composition of governing boards in 1947. In many respects he followed up on a study that Scott Nearing conducted in 1917. Nearing concluded, as did Beck 30 years later, that "the college and university boards are almost completely dominated by [businesspeople]. A new term must be coined to suggest the idea of an educational system owned and largely supported by the people but dominated by the business world—plutocratized education" (Beck, 1947, p. 9). Earl J. McGrath (1936) undertook a similar study by using the same manner of analysis and arrived at the same conclusion: "The control of higher education in America, both public and private, has been placed in the hands of a small group of the population: namely financiers and business people" (p. 266). Around the time of the Civil War, observed McGrath, the clergy accounted for close to 40% of membership on boards, but 70 years later, their numbers had dropped to less than 10%. Thomas, Pusser, and Slaughter (2002) continued this line of investigation in the late 20th century and came to similar conclusions. Duryea and Williams (2000) also presented a historical analysis of boards, and Holly Madsen (1997) published an AGB paper that discussed the composition of governing boards.

Conversely, one is hard-pressed to find an article on governance that does not mention an academic or faculty senate. Indeed, when one speaks of governance, the senate is often used as a synonym for governance, as if faculty senates are the only governance structure for higher education. Trow (1990), for example, wrote of senates as key (p. 23); Gilmour (1991b) argued that governance—the senate—was more effective than one presumed (p. 16); and Williams, Gore, Broches, and Lostoski (1987) noted that "the key to

successful faculty participation in policy probably lies in a sophisticated refinement of the representative assembly already found on some campuses—
the faculty senate" (p. 632). They went on to warn that if governance were
to remain stable, "faculty members will have to devote time and energy to
senate activities" (p. 632). Lee (1991) undertook an analysis of surveys of faculty attitudes toward campus governance and equated governance with senate involvement (p. 41). Thirty years ago an American Association for Higher
Education (AAHE) (1967) report rationalized that "faculty participation in
campus decision making requires formal arrangements through which faculty influence may be exercised" (p. 24), which assumed a formal structure
governed by the faculty. Richard Chait (2002) also did a study of the role of
tenure in governance and found that campuses with tenure had faculty who
were more active in governance. David Hollinger (2001) also has written op-
timistically about governance, saying, "[T]he Berkeley senate is one of the
most powerful in American higher education" (p. 30). Thus, the senate at
the research university has been almost exclusively the unit of analysis under
investigation.

Such an assumption, of course, is troubling for at least four reasons.
First, senates are a relatively new organizational structure, so to equate governance with a senate is to forget the historical basis for academic governance.
Second, academic senates often are discussed as they exist at private and public research universities when in reality more than half of academe does not
resemble such an organizational type. Third, to speak only of senates and
overlook boards is akin to speaking about governance in the United States
by analyzing the U.S. Senate and ignoring the House. And, finally, as noted,
even faculty participation has broadened considerably from simply a legislative forum such as a faculty senate. As I will elaborate on, a cultural framework guides the analyst about ways to think of governance so that
governance is more than simply one or another structure. Before we turn to
a discussion of a cultural model, however, I consider another framework that
has been utilized in studies of governance.

Constituencies as a Framework

Given the foregoing discussion, one ought not to be surprised that the group
that is most discussed with regard to its participation in governance is the
faculty. Perhaps most odd, however, is the paucity of research and discussion
about the role of students and external constituencies in governance. Except

for a brief burst of discussion in the 1960s, when students demanded a say in the running of the institution, students have been silent partners in academic life. The point is not merely that those who conduct research on higher education have fetishized their own role in governance, but that ignoring the student role in governance implicitly defines governance in a particular manner. Just as discussions of governance from one perspective or another assume that governance is important, when one studiously ignores a constituency, this assumes more than that the constituency "should" not have a role. By its absence, the point is made that it does not have a role.

The literature that exists about student governance is generally confined to student affairs journals. Student participation in governance refers to the activities of student government; there is no sense of shared governance insofar as the sharing is seen as a tripartite arrangement across the board, the administration, and the faculty. Students are defined as undergraduates, and the graduate student role in governance is neglected. Even in the 1960s, when individuals lobbied for a student voice in governance, the point was to add a student or two to a committee, not to give the students a structural voice akin to a faculty senate. Two points are worth mentioning here.

First, one ought not to overlook how Americentric the research has been on academic governance. If one looks abroad to either Latin America or Europe, there is a long tradition of including students in the governance processes of the institution. My suggestion is not to argue that students should be included in governance in one way or another, but that, within the United States, researchers have constructed governance processes in a particular way that more closely resemble corporate models of governance rather than those founded on principles of communality. Even the most inclusive of organizations, the AAUP (2001), has stated in its commentary:

> Ways should be found to permit significant student participation within the limits of attainable effectiveness. The obstacles to such participation are large and should not be minimized: inexperience, untested capacity, a transitory status which means that present action does not carry with it subsequent responsibility . . . (p. 267)

One need not be a literary theorist to translate such a comment as reflecting little role for students in the actual running of the institution. Student participation may impede "effectiveness." The obstacles are "large."

Students do not have experience in governance, they are untested, and because they will exit the institution within a matter of years, they are not responsible for carrying out the actions that are decided. Of course, one could raise related concerns with either the administration or the faculty. The average tenure of presidents is approximately five years, so the decisions they make are often not the ones they must carry out. Faculty leaders often come to such roles with little, if any, experience. If a prerequisite for leadership is that an individual not be "transitory," then presumably any number of professors or administrators would be unable to participate because successful academics are frequently on the move.

Again, the point is not to suggest that the path to student participation in the governance of an institution is easy or even warranted. However, one ought to acknowledge the socially constructed nature of this academic universe. For example, Deep Springs College has existed for close to a century in the California desert with a radical form of governance: students run the college. They choose the president, pick the faculty, and determine the curricula. Only the board of trustees faintly resembles what exists in most institutions (Tierney, 1993). Here, then, exists an institution that stands governance on its head. The assumptions of the AAUP document are flatly rejected, and if one were to study Deep Springs, one would need to discuss the role of students in the governance of the institution. Self-governance is a key precept, a raison d'être, of Deep Springs.

My second point, then, is that over the last generation there has been considerable discussion about the nature of inquiry. Broadly stated, history pertained to analyses of great men, not women, and minorities seemed not to exist if one were to read about any number of components of 19th-century America. My concern is similar when we look at the research on governance in higher education. If one is to look at such research, one needs to consider what exists, but also what—and who—is absent. Such a suggestion points up the theoretical frameworks upon which the research rests, and to this we now turn.

The Research Frames of Governance

What methodologies and theoretical frameworks have been employed when studying governance? The methodological question is simply answered. There have been virtually no national surveys of governance, although the AAUP did a study in 1971 that has recently been replicated (Kaplan, 2002), and another national survey was completed (Tierney & Minor, 2002). Most quantitative studies have been surveys of fewer than 200 faculty or administrators at an institution or two (e.g., Miller, McCormack, & Newman, 1996; Williams et al. 1987) or a randomized sample of an academic population no greater than 750 (Blackwell & Cistone, 1999; Drummond & Reitsch, 1995; Gilmour, 1991a, 1991b). Most quantitative studies have employed simple reporting techniques such as informing the reader that x percent of the faculty perceived governance one way, and y percent thought another way.

Qualitative studies also have been relatively meager. Individual case studies have used interviews as the main technique (Dykes, 1968), as have cross-site case studies (Eckel, 2000; Millett, 1978) that also employed interviews as the main data-gathering technique. Although their book has a much wider scope than simply governance, Leslie and Fretwell's (1996) in-depth case studies of 13 institutions had governance as one area of investigation. Schuster and associates (1994) conducted quasi-case studies for research pertaining to the role of cross-campus "strategic planning councils," and Lionel Lewis (2000) wrote a case history of the contretemps with the academic governing board at Adelphi University.

The overwhelming amount of writing, however, is based in neither qualitative nor quantitative methodologies. Instead, commissions and committees have written reports such as those of the AAUP and AGB. Former participants and combatants in governance have shared their experiences and reflections (e.g., Duderstadt, 2000a; Griffith, 1993; Hollinger, 2001; Wolvin, 1991), and numerous essayists with a great deal of perspective about higher education have offered their own opinions (Alfred, 1985; Keller, 1987; Longin, 2002; Pfnister, 1970).

A pessimistic conclusion that one could draw about the research is that the literature on shared governance is methodologically weak. Indeed, one wonders why an area that has drawn so much discussion and commentary does not have a richer empirical base from which to draw conclusions. Whereas national studies of student attitudes, retention, and faculty work habits abound, there is a very thin database to utilize about governance. An optimistic view is that a great deal of work awaits those who are searching for an area to investigate.

One might make a similar comment about the theoretical frameworks that authors have employed in studying academic governance; however, such a point is slightly off target. That is, one might argue that most of the articles, monographs, and books about governance in higher education are theoretically impoverished. Only a handful of studies have utilized explicit theoretical tools to diagnose a particular area of inquiry such as the role of the faculty senate. However, most of the texts have used one of two implicit theoretical frameworks: the collegial model or the bureaucratic model. Such a commentary is odd, given the wealth of frameworks that might be employed from business, public policy, sociology, and other disciplines. Additional analytic frameworks are the political model developed by Victor Baldridge in the 1970s and what Robert Birnbaum (1989) termed the cybernetic model. Nevertheless, most authors remain wedded to the bureaucratic and collegial approaches. A brief review of how each model diagnoses academic governance is useful.

The *bureaucratic model*, first articulated by Max Weber (1864–1920), assumes that decisions and planning take place by way of a coordinated division of labor, a standardization of rules and regulations, and a hierarchical chain of command (Baldridge, 1971; Hardy, 1990). Unlike traditional bureaucracies, in which supervision and centralization were typical, investigators of academic bureaucracies argued that colleges and universities functioned in a different manner. Bureaucracy in colleges and universities was legitimized in decentralized units such as departments. Power existed in a decentralized fashion through the preset assumptions that a socialized cadre—the faculty—had internalized before joining the academy.

Some argued that, in a professional bureaucracy, the standardization of skills did not occur by organizational rules, but by professional ideologies. The organization did not dictate that the academic needed to publish a specific set of articles or teach a particular number of classes—the profession did. A professional bureaucracy appeared as an oxymoron to some individuals, but, actually, academic organizations developed ways to function that incorporated both perspectives. On the one hand, the loosely coupled nature of an academic institution suited professionals who at best shared their allegiance to their disciplines with the institution; on the other hand, these professionals also needed standardized, predetermined processes for organizational decisions such as recruitment, tenure, and curricular reform.

The critics have pointed out that issues such as one's commitment to the organization and the amount of teaching one does are exactly why a return to bureaucratic processes is warranted. Those who advocate for a more formalized process of governance point out that organizational outcomes and quality have suffered because of the decentralized decision-making nature of the academy. Numerous critics have pointed out that solutions exist that will improve the quality of the institution—the removal of tenure, an increase in teaching, and the elimination of unproductive units are mentioned frequently—but such solutions are impossible because of the governance processes of the institution. The answer is a more centralized approach to decision making with greater power and authority at the presidential level (AGB, 1996). As Cary Nelson (1999) has noted, such approaches "consistently view the faculty largely as a resource to be 'managed,' as 'human capital' to be 'defined, directed, and deployed' with originality and attention to institutional mission" (p. B4). Richardson (1999), too, derided the movement toward bureaucratization and attributed such a desire to "obliviousness, indifference [and] hostility" (p. B9).

The apocalyptic warnings of scholars such as Nelson and Richardson are frequently in reaction to the more flamboyant attacks on academe such as those made by an errant trustee or legislator. Obviously, no serious scholar would argue that every individual who calls for more bureaucratic controls is ill willed or malevolent. However, two observations are pertinent. First, rhetoric often becomes heated when discussing possible changes in governance structures, whether one works from an explicit theoretical framework or not. Second, those who are most critical of a movement toward bureaucracy have as their implicit framework that of the collegium, to which we now turn.

The *collegial model* is a view of academic life that assumes that a community of scholars operates around notions of respect and consensus. Hamilton (1997) has pointed out that such an assumption works from a liberal, intellectual vantage point with regard to how knowledge creation works. Proponents of the collegial perspective argue that decisions are made through professional competence and authority rather than politics and rules. The loosely coupled and decentralized nature of the academy is well suited to such a framework. John Millett (1962), one of the earliest advocates of the collegium, nicely summarized the position by stating: "I do not believe that a structure of hierarchy is a desirable prescription for the organization of a college. . . . The concept of community presupposes an organization in which functions are differentiated . . . through a dynamic of consensus" (p. 5).

Although such a view of the academy has numerous proponents, very little empirical literature supports the notion that the academy is now, or has ever been, a collegium. As Baldridge (1971) noted, "Frequently it is obvious that the discussions of a collegium are more a lament for paradise lost than a description of present reality" (p. 7). Nevertheless, the collegial model remains remarkably popular with authors. Changes in the structure and work of academic life are seen as attacks on the collegial model, and responses are often based on the desire for a return to the status quo—even if that status quo never really existed. In a lament for the changes that are currently taking place in the academy, for example, Mary Burgan (1998), general secretary of the AAUP, wrote, "I cannot believe that the solution to our present problems is to turn our backs on such an ideal of community" (p. 20). Similarly, Keetjie Ramo (1997) critiqued the proposals for reform of governance and found that "the arguments used to question the faculty's role in governance do not hold up well" (p. 43). In other words, one ought to return to the notion of collegiality, community, and, hence, shared governance.

The *political model* took hold in the late 1960s and early 1970s. Baldridge (1971) rejected the forced choice one had to make between a college or university as a bureaucracy or as a consensus-driven association of scholars. Conflict, give-and-take, and bargaining, rather than routinized processes and consensus, were what existed in academe. In some respects, such a model provided a very useful tool to analyze academic processes. Especially during times of duress, such as the student movement in the 1960s, an analysis of how issues were resolved inevitably took on a political tint. Collective bargaining, demands from external constituencies, and system-wide bargains are additional examples where the political lens may be a useful analytic tool.

However, as Hardy (1990) has noted, the problem of the political model is that it seems to incorporate all organizational action and all theoretical models under its rubric (p. 399). The entire organizational world becomes political. The bureaucratic, collegial, and related models get incorporated into the political model. And yet, the political model did not seem especially useful for studying the more ordinary, mundane processes that tended to dominate academic life, rather than the more crisis-laden actions that had made the political model possible. After an initial burst of use by scholars, the model appears to be underused, rather than discarded. On the one hand, those who subscribe to the bureaucratic model are more concerned with practical concerns, so a model that diagnoses, rather than prescribes, is insufficient. On the other hand, the proponents of the collegial model are concerned with describing how the academic world should be, rather than how it is, so a political model is also of little use.

The *cybernetic model*, championed by Robert Birnbaum, is the most recent proposal to dominate the theoretical landscape. Birnbaum (1989) argued the following:

> The cybernetic paradigm integrates existing models by suggesting how bureaucratic, collegial, political, and anarchical subsystems function simultaneously in colleges and universities of all kinds to create self-correcting institutions. The cybernetic paradigm posits that organization control systems can be described in terms of sensing mechanisms and negative feedback loops that collectively monitor changes from acceptable levels of functioning and that activate forces that return institutions to their previous stable state. These self-correcting (cybernetic) processes function as institutional "thermostats." (p. 239)

Because the model is relatively new, it has not attracted a great deal of analysis or critique. One observation is that the research Birnbaum conducted to produce this model derived from studies of college presidents and decision making, rather than of academic governance. The model has relatively little to say about the role, for example, of faculty or boards in decision making. Instead, the model helps college presidents and administrators think through how they might manage the organization in a more organic and flexible manner. Although one conceivably might be able to derive some idea about what to expect in a cybernetic organization from faculty, trustees, or other groups, very little empirical work has been done that delineates such a finding.

A second observation is that the cybernetic model might be applied more fruitfully in organizations that are doing relatively well or are on stable ground. As Birnbaum (1989) noted, the adage, "If it's working, keep doing it. If it's not working, stop doing it. If you don't know what to do, don't do anything," is appropriate for the cybernetic leader (p. 251). Such advice, of course, flies in the face of organizations that face disruptive technologies. We have learned, for example, from the work of Christensen (1997) and Frank and Cook (1996), that technologies such as the Internet have remarkable power to change a marketplace. Equilibrium in a dynamic environment cannot be achieved, and those who seek it are those who will be at risk. If one accepts the assertion that academic organizations are in dynamic environments that necessitate changes, then the maxim to keep doing what one has been doing is ill-advised.

An additional framework that is not so much a theoretical model but a way of thinking about decision making and governance was first proposed by Mortimer and McConnell (1978). In a thoughtful piece about how the processes of governance might function more effectively, the authors posited that various stages of consultation were necessary. Subsequent authors (e.g., Hardy, Langley, Mintzberg, & Rose, 1983) elaborated on the work of Mortimer and McConnell by pointing out the importance of early consultation, the role of temporality in decision making, how one uses feedback and communicates to multiple constituencies, and the import of comparative and evaluative criteria. The assumption of these authors was that shared governance is necessary for sustained, successful reform, but their critiques generally do not subscribe to any particular theoretical framework.

Thus, I have outlined four frameworks that have been used to study governance. Analysts who use a *historical* framework primarily look at the varying stages of governance over time. Those who use a *contexts and structures* framework emphasize the setting in which governance takes place and investigate different decision-making bodies such as an academic senate. Students of the *constituency* framework look at who participates. Finally, proponents of a *research* framework in general employ bureaucratic, collegial, or political models. Each framework has particular strengths such as the ability to look over time at how governance has changed in the historical framework, or to focus in-depth analysis at a particular constituency such as the faculty. The frames may serve as filters through which to think about shared governance.

The challenge for students of higher education research is threefold. First, the theoretical models that have been used appear to be of limited utility. In particular, even though the bureaucratic and collegial models remain the popular lenses through which to view academic governance, the models do not provide an accurate, holistic portrait of the environments in which colleges and universities currently exist. Second, the empirical base on which most current work on governance has been written is thin, to say the least. At a time when quantitative and qualitative measures have become increasingly sophisticated, one expects to find more thoughtful uses of different techniques. Third, the kind of academic organization one needs in the 21st century is a new kind of institution. I am not suggesting that academic traditions be dropped in a simpleminded fashion, or that colleges and universities as we have known them be abandoned in favor of for-profit or corporate organizations. However, academic organizations have been superb at functioning in a stable, closed environment. The current contexts, however, are the opposite—the environment is unstable and open to market forces. For the first time in its history, the American college faces competitors in an unregulated, competitive market. What might these changes augur for academic governance? I address this question in the following section before turning to a cultural model of shared governance.

Rethinking Shared Governance in the Innovating Organization

Colleges and universities with active faculties frequently will have developed detailed handbooks and bylaws pertaining to governance. The bylaws of the James E. Beasley School of Law at Temple University (n.d.), for example, clearly state the expectation that the faculty be consulted or involved in most institutions' decisions. Anyone familiar with academe will readily comprehend the sentiments of such a statement as a call for shared governance. The problem, of course, arises not with a generic call for shared governance, but with the shared understanding of the words of the sentence. Should faculty really be involved in "most" institutional decisions? Who decides how "varying" the consultation is with each decision? How "involved" should the "faculty" be in these decisions; who determines how to define the "faculty"? The questions are not indicative of loose wording by an errant author; many individuals will have wildly different interpretations of the ideas, rather than the words.

Some will say that the purpose of academic senates, school councils, and departmental meetings is precisely to deal with "most" institutional decisions; others will point out it is absurd to think that any representative forum could deal with the array of decisions that need to be made on a daily basis. Some administrators and faculty will point out that "institutional" decisions are not simply administrative actions, such as whether to repave a parking lot, but decisions that affect the organization. Still other individuals will argue that the decision to pave a parking lot actually should have faculty input. A strong leader may consult with a kitchen cabinet that includes faculty on the direction he or she intends to take, and the president will then say that faculty were involved in the decision; others will argue that only if the senate votes on an issue is there adequate faculty consultation.

A satisfactory determination of how an institution's participants might deal with both everyday and long-term issues goes to the heart of what is meant by "shared governance." I have suggested that in order to define shared governance so that such questions might be answered, one needs to come to terms with the multiple constituencies, contexts, and sociocultural environments in which an organization exists. At present, the field has neither adequate data nor theoretical models to explain how to approach answering these questions. Insofar as I am more concerned with coming to terms with an understanding of shared governance for the 21st century than with simply a historical exegesis about shared governance, the challenge is to understand the cartography within which academe exists in the early 21st century.

In 1970 Allan Pfnister wrote, "With the increase in size and complexity of the academy, it has been necessary to add a management function. Yet faculties hold to the tradition of the collegium and tend to become anti-organization and anti-administration when they feel that they have less opportunity to influence directly the qualities of the institution" (p. 432). More recently, Ramo (1997) rejected the assumption of a need for greater administrative authority by deriding the notion that "if old-fashioned bureaucracy is good for the Acme Widget Manufacturing Company, then it is undoubtedly good for Midwest State University" (p. 40).

Both points are important because they underscore the importance of context. Those who want less formal faculty involvement in governance often speak of the complexity of the 21st-century university (Duderstadt, 2000b). Those who reject such an assertion frequently point out that such arguments have always been used to lessen faculty participation in governance—evidence the comment Pfnister made 30 years ago. Similarly, Ramo painted a stark picture by comparison: who wants a university to become a widget company? Rather than reject out of hand that the organization is too complex for shared authority, or accept that because of the complexity of organizational life, shared governance is no longer viable, I turn to a consideration of the current contexts of academic life. I move away from the

creation of a "straw man" by assuming universities are about to become widget factories insofar as only the most pedestrian of observers call for returns
to "old-fashioned bureaucracy." Increasingly, what one finds in organizational life is a more nuanced sense of decision making that may well suit the
needs of academic governance in the 21st century.

Disruptive Technologies in Traditional Organizations

In *The Innovator's Dilemma*, Christensen (1997) argued that new technologies sustained or disrupted an industry. Audiovisual equipment or the microphone might be seen as a sustaining technology for teaching and
learning at colleges and universities. Both technologies helped improve the
organization, yet did not disrupt the normal flow of activities. Teachers
still taught in the same classrooms in the same manner, albeit with more
advanced tools than a blackboard and a piece of chalk. The concept of
"teacher" did not change, and the "student" still needed to function in the
same way as he or she did before the invention of audiovisual equipment or
the microphone.

A disruptive technology is more significant. The new technology provides different benefits, creates new markets, and threatens existing ones.
One might consider the Internet, distance learning, and the World Wide
Web as disruptive technologies for academic organizations. True, the Internet and the Web might be seen as sustaining technologies. The teacher
who once provided class notes as handouts now simply puts them on the
Web. The class now may post one another's comments to a listserv rather
than reading to one another in a face-to-face study group. However, the potential for disruption is vast. The traditional idea of the "teacher" might be
dispensed with if the curriculum is entirely online. The assumption that students need to take a class at a specific location and at a particular time may
be discarded.

Teachers always assumed that their class notes were their own intellectual
property. The consumers of those notes were the few hundred students who
received instruction from the professor. If the professor wrote a textbook to
teach the class, then he or she benefited from the royalties of the text. Electronic technologies disrupt such basic assumptions. In a world where the
curriculum in a professor's class may not reach hundreds of students in a
classroom building, but thousands of students in multiple venues around the

world, who owns the intellectual property becomes a question. Of consequence, who receives the royalties becomes subject to debate. The result is that a technology has the potential not only to change but to revolutionize an industry—in this case, higher education.

An interesting aspect of disruptive technologies is that they begin with subpar performance or quality, and they are frequently expensive. Established companies usually do not develop disruptive technologies precisely because the technologies at the outset are not equivalent to what the companies currently offer their customers. The established companies have a customer base that expects a particular level of quality at a predetermined cost. Start-up companies that have a new idea and little to lose are the locales where disruptive technologies are usually born. The new technology will create new markets rather than improve current ones, so the start-ups are not competing against well-established companies. Start-up companies have room to experiment, innovate, and improve; if they are successful, they have a head start on utilizing a revolutionary technology that will appeal to an enormous customer base. The computer is the most obvious example. Those consumers who used manual typewriters readily adapted to the sustaining technology that created electric typewriters. The companies that manufactured typewriters saw the rationale for their customers with a new improved technology. However, the names of computer software companies are not Olivetti or Smith-Corona because the computer was a disruptive technology. Some young fellows worked in their garage and involved customers who were intrigued by the possibilities of a computer; they improved their product, lowered their prices, and the rest, as they say, is history.

New companies utilize the disruptive technology in large part because they have less to lose. New markets emerge, costs go down, and quality goes up. Lloyd Armstrong (2000) observed,

> At this point, mainstream customers perceive the disruptive technology as providing a superior product, because it brings additional benefits compared to the established technology. Given its lower cost structure, the disruptive technology then rapidly displaces the established products, and leads to a revolutionary change in the industry. (p. 22)

Such changes do not occur over a century because, if they did, it would enable traditional companies to adapt gradually. Disruptive technologies are more like a tidal wave that washes over rigid organizational structures that are ill prepared to adapt and innovate.

The Buffeted Organization

If disruptive technologies were the only impact on higher education, the implications for governance would be significant. However, colleges and universities are being buffeted by multiple forces. Changing demographics are more significant today than at any time in the last century. Students enter and exit postsecondary institutions with greater frequency than ever before; "retention" takes on a different meaning when students do not "drop out" but instead decide to leave for a time and return—perhaps to a different institution—later. The nature of employment is being reconfigured so that "work" is no longer considered as lifetime employment at one company; employees increasingly approach organizations as "free agents." Academics, already more wedded to their disciplines than their institution, have even weaker loyalties to the organization.

A by-product of the Internet is the explosion in knowledge, the reconfiguration of disciplines, and the need for specialization. Globalization affects markets, which, in turn, affect educational providers. The fastest-growing sectors in postsecondary education are those organizations that are not traditional colleges and universities. Postsecondary institutions are now in a competitive market where they need to compete with an array of providers. Each of these points underscores how differently one might define "complexity" today than one would have in 1970, much less 1950. Previous analysts thought of complexity as the array of units and departments that a "complex" organization needed to provide to the consumer. Although that internal definition of complexity has remained, the definition of the consumer has multiplied, and the external environment has made the organization itself a more complex interpretive undertaking. That is, a generation ago, if someone said, "college" or "university," a particular image came to mind. Such an image is no longer clear.

A change in one area presages changes in others. A new definition of what one thinks of as faculty work suggests that employment contracts and tenure will be redefined. Changes in the labor market are much more complicated in a mature industry such as higher education that has multiple sectors, multiple demands, and multiple interpretations. The implications of a disruptive technology, for example, have different implications for an elite research university and a public state college. How a low-status professional school such as education reacts to changes will also differ, whether or not the school is at a struggling small liberal arts college or a comprehensive university. As David Collis (2000) has observed, "Part of the problem . . . is that many items are interrelated. It is hard to distinguish what are the truly independent and underlying drivers of change and establish a clear logic of cause and effect. As a result, it is difficult to cleanly determine how each of these forces will change higher education" (p. 103). The assumption, of course, is not *if* change will occur, but *how* higher education will change.

If one accepts even part of the thumbnail sketch that I have provided, then to claim that the postsecondary organization is going through significant contextual changes and is being buffeted by external demands, constraints, and forces ought not to be thought of as the cries of academic Chicken Littles. There will be winners and losers, and as Frank (2000) has succinctly claimed, there will be a "winner-take-all trend in higher education where success breeds success and failure breeds failure" (p. 3). One also ought to see that those who subscribe to bureaucratic calls for governance at such a time run the risk of irrelevance. Simply recreating organizational life a half-century ago is not helpful in an environment framed by disruptive technologies, changing demographics, never-before-seen competition, and other forces. If anything, the opposite sentiment seems warranted. Rather than a lethargic call for the reinstallation of bureaucracy, those who study the changes that are taking place tend to advocate a new governance structure. Collis (2000) has written that a strategic necessity "that I believe has become even more important [is] speed" (p. 123). He goes on to argue the following:

> This implies that universities should attach a great urgency to debates about their future. Rather than sitting back and observing how the market develops, university presidents and administrators should be proactively determining the future of their institutions. Otherwise they will be condemned to be the bystanders that get swept away in the tides of change. (p. 123)

Armstrong (2000) arrived at essentially the same conclusion and pointed out the implications for shared governance. He writes, "Because the private sector can move rapidly and with very significant financial resources, the resulting pressures on universities and colleges could push them to act much more quickly than is usually possible within the tradition of shared governance" (p. 24). The point, of course, is not simply the speed with which an organization's participants make a decision. A quickly made poor decision is as futile as one made slowly. The assumption, however, is that the complexity of the current environment demands thoughtful analyses leading to deliberate decisions that position the organization to compete in ways that have been unnecessary until the dawn of the 21st century.

Accordingly, calls for the reinstallation of bureaucracy or the reduction of the argument that one's opponents want to create a production model for the academy belies the complexity of the current climate. At the same time, the leisurely pace demanded of a consensual approach appears impossible if one wants to create an innovating organization. Perhaps an apt analogy might be the distinction between a large, oceangoing vessel and a sailboat. Colleges and universities are traditional vessels, and they have weathered one or another storm without too much concern about the external environment. Ships such as the *Titanic* were not able to be either agile or adaptive. Their success came through their strength. Sailboats are able to shift with the wind; they are buffeted by the seas, but they are able to respond, and a skilled team is able to reach its destination. A call for a commander who has the skills of a ship's captain is as mistaken as assuming that the only metaphor for an organization is that of a ship. Obviously, the movement from a mentality that assumes organizational action is determined by a rigid plan to one that is more interpretive is not a simple transformation that occurs according to a predetermined set of instructions. What, then, might be the lineaments of a solution?

The Innovating Organization

Letts, Ryan, and Grossman (1999) have observed that "'innovative' often means little more than 'well implemented'" (p. 18). Programs that stand out are ones that are well implemented, but there is little sense of whether they work. Outcomes certainly matter; however, in academic organizations, the focus has generally been on a static concept of innovation. Someone creates an innovation in an organization, and then it is replicated. Or a new concept is implemented after a multiyear review. Consider, for example, changes to general education, intellectual property rights, or the role of part-time faculty. Each change is looked on as a unique idea that is successful if it is implemented. If one believes the comments made in the previous section, however, rather than a static notion of *innovation*, what the governance process needs to be attuned to is the ability for innovativeness—the capacity to innovate repeatedly (Light, 1998) and at the same time maintain what Clark (1998) has labeled a "steering core" (p. 5). In a previous work (Tierney, 1999), I have talked about the twin challenges of maintaining an organizational identity on the one hand and building an experimental environment on the other. If an organization's governance structure is geared toward maintaining the status quo, then in the kind of environment I have just outlined, the campus will face great difficulties. At the same time, if the organization's governance structures are set up to enable the college or university merely to adapt to the environment, then the campus will ultimately run into trouble. The challenge is to create processes and structures of governance that enable academic organizations to create and sustain an experimental environment while at the same time holding onto core values.

Obviously, such a question touches a variety of issues that have become the buzzwords of recent years—total quality improvement, high performance, and restructuring, to name but a few. My point here is not to analyze any of these thorny concepts but to focus on how the governing structures of traditional colleges and universities might reorient their processes to ensure that innovation is fostered. In doing so, I accept neither that "shared" governance is dead nor that the academic world is so complex that the only route to agile decision making is through a reenergized form of martial law in which the president makes all the decisions.

Instead, in what follows, I work from a cultural perspective that has five provisional tenets pertaining to governance. In a 1990 article about university governance, Hardy noted that "the new direction of research is toward culture" (p. 405). However, other than an article or two (e.g., Lee, 1991), a discussion that employed culture as a theoretical model for diagnosing governance has been absent; as might be expected, there also has been a paucity of empirical studies that worked from a cultural perspective when studying governance. My purpose, then, is to sketch the outlines of an approach as a trial of some ideas that might be examined and revised or refuted. To encourage analysis, I discuss these points as assertions so that they can be proved or disproved.

Organizational Culture and Shared Governance

The underlying tenet of a cultural perspective is that one needs to constantly interpret the environment and the organization to internal and external constituencies. Organizations and the environments in which they exist neither come predefined nor are they capable of instantaneous redefinition as if the contexts in which they exist are irrelevant. Although some organizational cultures may have had bureaucratic, collegial, or cybernetic governing mechanisms, what I am suggesting here is that those who think of their environment and organization from a cultural perspective will look at governance from a *different* vantage point. If a key determinant of governance is that of interpretation, then how one thinks of governance changes. In particular, five precepts arise based on previous definitions of organizational culture (Tierney, 1988, 1991). As I will discuss, the precepts are tightly connected to one another; one cannot employ one and ignore another because a cultural perspective assumes that an organization's culture is pervasive. All acts are interpretive and dynamic. To assume that one act—such as a speech—is a symbolic event and another—the budget—is not is to mistake the meaning of culture. Hence, one needs to think of governance and its components as symbolic and interpretive.

Define Decisional Outcomes and Purpose

What is the purpose of governance? All too frequently, governance has been discussed without a sense of the reason why one has constructed a governance structure in a particular format. The process of governance has been treated as an end in itself. Instead, an organization's participants need to think of governance as a symbolic and interpretive process devised to achieve particular outcomes.

Outcomes are not always quantifiable. The advancement and protection of academic freedom, for example, may not be readily quantified. A rise in academic quality, however, may lend itself to measurable criteria. Both outcomes lend themselves to particular ways to approach governance. A concern for academic freedom suggests that faculty ought to be involved in the processes taken to ensure its protection. In traditional colleges and universities, faculty also will be involved in defining the criteria for academic quality. As Martin Trow's quotation suggested earlier, an additional role of shared governance might be to insulate the organization from political interference. Again, such an outcome is less easily quantified and most likely pertains more to public institutions than to private ones. Thus, outcomes are context dependent and may be evaluated in a number of ways.

This symbolic aspect of governance pertains to those who are involved and those who get left out as well as the outcomes one uses to determine the effectiveness of the governance process. In a buffeted organization one needs to be able to make agile decisions of importance to the organization's participants. Such ability depends upon how the organization's participants interpret their environment. Simply because structures exist is not a sufficient reason for claiming that governance works. What are the indicators one might employ to think about in judging the strengths and weaknesses of the governance processes of a particular institution? The answer to such a question is one step beyond simply bemoaning or celebrating that an organization has an academic senate, faculty involvement, or a strong board of trustees.

Instead, the point pertains to how one might gauge the effectiveness of shared governance. If a cultural framework for governance is in a constant state of creation/re-creation, then, of necessity, ongoing reflective dialogues and debates ought to occur over who is involved in what particular format with how much authority in an institution. The collegial assumption of consensus is dropped in favor of a cultural model that accepts the notion of creative conflict. Cultures are not consensual; different individuals and groups will have different perspectives. Insofar as cultures are not monolithic, it stands to reason that governance structures also will not be uniform. The challenge for researchers is to investigate the multiple venues employed in reaching a decision and to determine whether these venues are effective in enabling the organization to achieve its goals.

Define Venues of Decision Making and Units of Analysis

A similar effort ought to be made with regard to the venues of decision making and the units of analysis. As has been outlined, most discussions of faculty governance inevitably equate faculty deliberations with the academic senate. And yet, faculty deliberate in multiple venues with multiple levels of input and authority. A structural focus is only one way to analyze governance. Additional ways are to investigate the multiple arenas where people become involved and to look at specific issues to see who is involved or not on a particular topic. The challenge here is to move away from a linear and hierarchical chain of decision making and toward a more protean analysis that accepts that not all decisions are equal, not all decisions require multiple levels of review, not all decisions necessitate a hierarchical chain of command, and not all decisions will be reached by a faculty or a board having veto power. Some observers of higher education organizations will comment that I am merely stating the obvious: of course, the board of regents is not involved in every decision; of course, all decisions are not equal. However, if one returns to an earlier section of this text, we find precisely such assumptions about faculty power and authority. Recall the comment about the need for faculty to be involved in "most" decisions. What one needs to do is determine the level of input and then ensure that varying levels of participation occur in a systematic and thoughtful manner. Clearly, a return to a centralized hierarchical structure is not conducive to the kinds of changes I am suggesting for a buffeted organization. A risk is that how one perceives a particular group's input will vary from constituent to constituent. Without centralization, different groups will make decisions independent of one another because they feel it is in their domain of influence.

A crucial issue is to define the domain and nature of influence by different constituents. The domain of influence refers to the levels of power and control a group has on a particular issue, such as standards for evaluating teaching or policies pertaining to intellectual property. The nature of a group's influence considers the varying ways by which influence is exerted. Do the faculty have veto power over defining teaching standards, or do they merely have input? There is not a certain, singular response. In a dynamic environment the culture of the organization is constantly interpreted and reinterpreted so that how one institution equitably decides such questions may differ from how another organization does so. All too often, however, the assumption has been that governance is a one-size-fits-all framework that may be replicated from one institution to the next. Governance, however, is the product of an interaction between cosmopolitan academic norms and localized cultural norms. The lineaments of a cultural strategy need to be outlined, and then the organization's participants allowed to fill in the answers. Without a sense of organizational identity, a decentralized style of decision making such as ought to occur in a buffeted organization will deteriorate into a loosely affiliated federation in which the parts are tangential to one another and the culture erodes.

Define the Core Identity

As one defines the purposes of the processes of shared governance and implements a radically decentralized process, of necessity one must have a clear sense of organizational identity. I have argued elsewhere (Tierney, 1998, 1999) about the overall importance of institutional identity, but in particular, if governance is to improve and move away from a bureaucratic or a collegial model, then an organization's participants ought to have a sense about the core values of the institution.

As Clark (1998) noted, "Strong cultures are rooted in strong practices. As ideas and practices interact, the cultural or symbolic side of the university becomes particularly important in cultivating institutional identity and distinctive reputation" (p. 7). Curiously, some have assumed that a strong culture is one that is wedded to the past and resistant to change. However, as Clark commented, the reverse is also possible—if not mandatory. To create an innovating environment, one does not need to revert to calls for strong presidential leadership or try to create an entrepreneurial climate in which tradition is disparaged. Instead, the challenge is to understand what cultural elements are vital to the core identity of the organization and use those elements to enhance dynamic participation in shared governance. An innovating organization has a culture that enables its governance structure to foment change.

That is, in a dynamic environment where an organization's participants seek to encourage innovation, one needs to view the governance processes as emergent and fluid rather than as developed and static. Structures will continually adapt. Any a priori notions that shared governance is equated with an academic senate, or that governance is confined to the trinity of faculty, trustees, and administration, are eschewed in favor of a more protean analysis of what constitutes governance. A strong organizational identity that is widely shared and believed is necessary. Leslie and Fretwell (1996) nicely summarized this point:

> Successful organizations seem to be good at continuous adaptation, seem to have strong cultures, and seem to enjoy well-developed communication skills (both internally and externally). They form strong internal value systems that serve as compasses and filter information from a wide variety of

sources through that value system. They do not make "strategic" decisions in the old linear/rational way but sense and flow in a continuous process of growth, change and reimagining. (p. 109)

An organization without an identity is often one whose mission is ill defined, programs continue to be added because the core is unclear, and resources are sprinkled across the multiple units within the organization. Frequently, there is a great deal of discussion about the processes of governance, again, as if these processes are outcomes. When governance becomes a main focal point, then the organization is unsure about its direction, where it wants to go, and how it should get there. The mistake is to obsess about governance, void of a discussion about institutional and governance-related outcomes.

In a related point, a common flaw for those who want to create change is to assume that change occurs through a linear process. First one assesses the environment, then one consults with particular individuals, then one draws up a plan, and, finally, the plan is implemented. Organizational identity does not enter a cultural undertaking as the first or third or final element. Each of these points, instead, is interlocked in cycles with one another. They feed, support, or distract from one another, and as the entire entity is in a state of constant change and permutation, so are each of the points. What is often overlooked is that, because humans are interpretive beings, they interpret not only the large aspects of an organization, such as its mission, but also the microscopic components of the organization. Such a reinterpretation—how the campus decides about a particular issue, for example, or who is involved in the decision—relates to the broader understandings of the organization itself.

Focus on the Communicative Processes of Governance

As Leslie and Fretwell (1996) cogently argued when they wrote against linear-rational approaches to strategic planning, "Change in colleges and universities comes when it happens in the trenches; what faculty and students do is what the institution becomes. It does not happen because a committee or a president asserts a new idea" (p. 110). Unfortunately, most research on governance reverts to old-fashioned notions of power, so "where the buck stops" is the one who has the authority. If the buck does not pass by the faculty or end on the desk in the boardroom, then the assumption is that governance is not shared. But governance in a decentralized 21st-century organization needs to be more than a simple check of who gets to vote and who is denied the opportunity.

Shared governance does not result from formal allocations of spheres of responsibility and authority (Trow, 1990, p. 24). Instead, informal arrangements and processes need to be interpreted by the academic collective about the relative weights given to different academic bodies in different decisions. Strategic governance is more an ongoing communicative process that works in organizations where participants trust one another and understand the identity that is trying to be cultivated. Formalized governance occurs in systems where there is a lack of trust and the collective has little sense of institutional purpose and ideology.

In a system where shared governance functions effectively, communication is key. At a time when organizations are buffeted by the winds of change, and where decentralization is encouraged, ongoing communication about the institution's identity and direction is essential. Who communicates to whom is again symbolic of the nature of governance. If the president is the only individual who sends out messages, one symbol is sent; in an organization where the faculty have ongoing discussions with academic staff and students about the nature of the organization, another message is sent. Without systematic efforts at communication the system freezes.

Determine the Effectiveness of Governance Processes in Enabling Decisions to Occur

Although a strong core is essential, and the ability to communicate that core is equally important, one also has to focus on how symbolic structures and processes get defined, carried out, and evaluated in the "real" world. That is, although where a parking lot gets placed may be a core issue over identity on one campus at one point, it is foolhardy to claim that such issues rise to the level of major cultural issues of organizational identity for all campuses all the time. This point is important because assumptions about the organization's culture generally work from a macro perspective when the opposite is more likely to happen. Authors assume that one or another symbolic act takes place because it reinforces the general tenets of the culture. From this perspective, ideology is all encompassing and inscribes meaning in all organizational action.

The opposite takes place: organizational actions provide meaning about the general tenets of the culture. To be sure, at times a particular theme or ideology pervades most aspects of the academic organization. A conservative Christian university, for example, may decide that what people wear is inappropriate, or it may define particular kinds of behavior such as coed dorms as inappropriate, even immoral. And yet, even at such an institution, not every action is a major signifier of the culture. However, the manner in which individuals work with one another, the way they decide issues, the formal structure of governance, and the like provide clues about the culture. Indeed, more often than not, individuals find meaning not from broad sweeping statements or events, but from the routine, microscopic aspects of everyday life.

As I noted in the first section, if there is one issue that individuals at all types of colleges and universities have bemoaned about campus governance, it is the efficiency, speed, and organization with which academic governance functions (Kezar & Eckel, 2002). Administrators feel stymied. Faculty feel their time is often wasted. The culture of an organization need not be one of governance by conversation (Tierney, 1983) in which decisions are endlessly delayed and the assumption is that the summer months are idle. Instead, one needs to diagnose how to improve the cultural processes that are in place to enable smoother, more efficient decision making. The assertion of administrative prerogative on peripheral issues is not a problem in an academic community that is based on trust, ongoing communication, and a clear identity.

The challenge is threefold. First, if the other cultural precepts are not clearly delineated, it is impossible to articulate whether the governance processes are functioning efficiently. In unstable environments, individuals are likely to demand structure if they are unsure of where the organization is heading or if an atmosphere of distrust exists. Second, if the organization remains wedded to a collegial model of consensus that was articulated a half-century ago, any individual will be able to filibuster or delay a decision simply because he or she disagrees. The processes of governance need to be fluid enough to move issues to a conclusion, while at the same time advancing, rather than stifling, communication. Third, in a dynamic system, the assignment of issues to different groups and venues becomes critical. Rather than assume that there is one best system for decision making, the community needs to draw upon the multiple venues that are possible to garner responsible input. Ultimately, an academic community needs to foment active involvement so that individuals are talking and thinking about the issues that confront the organization rather than about the processes one might use to discuss those issues. A successful governance process is one in which multiple constituencies have been involved in the main problems that confront the college or university. An unsuccessful campus is one where structures exist, but because of angst or alienation, no one participates or the dialogue focuses on the structures rather than the issues and problems.

Conclusion: The Next Generation of Research

I began by outlining the paucity of research that exists on a critically important topic. I noted that the manner in which governance has been studied is primarily in four frameworks: historical, structural, constituency-focused, and research-based. I then critiqued the research based on the current conditions that exist in academe and suggested that a cultural model might be a more appropriate way to analyze governance.

From this perspective, governance is a process and an outcome. Governance provides the foundation upon which organizations may prosper or fail. Governance is also little more than what a foundation is to a house; it is the individuals who make of that house a home. Governance is a mixture of academic cultural norms that have been built up over time and the localized cultural norms of a specific institution. Governance is more than merely an organizational chart that maps decision making; governance occurs in multiple venues. Accordingly, five avenues for research appear ripe for investigation.

Data Matter

If there is one particular need with regard to governance, it is the collection and analysis of data. Surveys will be able to provide broad-based understandings of how governance functions in colleges and universities as well as gauge the perceptions of different constituencies. Longitudinal data will be most useful to track the changes that occur over time. Case studies, interviews, and ethnographies are likely to provide in-depth understanding to individuals' perceptions of governance. Qualitative methodologists also will be able to sketch contextual issues so that readers might be able to understand the rationales for why particular changes have taken place.

If there is a caution, it is twofold. On the one hand, what the field needs less of are exhortations and lamentations about the state of governance from either those who want more administrative authority or those who perceive the demise of shared governance. Although such articles have served a purpose, they are identified more accurately as op-ed pieces for newspapers than as research. On the other hand, researchers need to move beyond their own campuses in their efforts. A case study of a senate, for example, where the researcher has been involved presents all sorts of methodological shortcomings, just as a survey of one's colleagues will have a circumscribed utility.

Context Matters

This text has focused on institutions where most of the writing has been done about academic governance: four-year colleges and universities. Although a great deal remains to be done in this arena, broad swaths of territory remain virtually ignored. Community colleges account for almost half of the population of postsecondary institutions, yet they are the least studied. Although most community colleges are public and frequently part of a system, there is little reason why the internal governance mechanisms for two-year institutions are not investigated. More important, as constituencies from the external environment have raised expectations and make increased demands on community colleges, a fruitful line of research is to see how a community college's governance procedures respond.

The fastest-growing sector of academe is the arena of for-profit and non-traditional institutions. These institutions, such as DeVry, the University of Phoenix, the Keck Graduate Institute, and Cardean University, have vastly different arrangements for governance. Academe is currently facing the greatest increase in innovative organizations since the 1960s. The experiments of the 1960s were watched closely and written about in great detail (Grant & Riesman, 1978). The opposite is currently true with the innovations that are taking place. Researchers need to broaden their horizons, stop looking at only institutions where they work, and begin looking at alternative organizational types. The purpose of such research is not to support or condemn such growth, but to analyze it in an objective manner.

Although nontraditional institutions are the fastest-growing sector in academe, the largest number of students remain in statewide systems of higher education. The literature on state systems of higher education, however, is virtually devoid of research about the interstices of governance. The state governance literature generally analyzes how states shift from one system to another, or how coordinating boards differ from state to state. Longitudinal studies are virtually absent, and a discussion of the roles of different constituencies in state systems of higher education is nonexistent. There is, for example, no research on the role of the faculty on a state board, much less that of students or other constituencies.

There is also very little research on the impact of collective bargaining on academic governance. Just as governance is successful in some public institutions and not in others, collective bargaining presumably has successful and unsuccessful examples of working within traditional governance structures. The dynamics of how collective bargaining functions at an institution have vast implications for the future of academic governance inasmuch as the movement seems to be toward greater unity of participation of multiple constituencies on campuses.

People Matter

Research on governance has been reduced to a triangle of constituencies—trustees, administrators, and faculty. Of those three, the least discussed group is the trustees, and the greatest number of articles refer to faculty. When research has been done about faculty, the definition has been focused on full-time, tenure-track faculty. However, the fastest-growing groups on some campuses are either non-tenure-track or part-time faculty. What is their role in the governance process? How does participation function for part-time and adjunct faculty, who are not at the top of the academic ladder and are often perceived as second-class citizens? There is no small amount of irony that, at a time when faculty in various academic disciplines have focused their energies on studying groups who have been excluded or ignored in fields such as history, literature, and political science, within the academy, those same groups that have been marginalized remain ignored.

Although a great deal of research remains to be done with regard to understanding the faculty's role in governance, the fastest-growing group in academe is the academic staff. Professional staff who are non-faculty fall into the interstices of categories. They are not faculty; they are not administrators; they are not classified staff; they are not students. And their growth has been enormous over the last decade. Their role in governing the institution needs to be investigated both for what is occurring and for how they have changed the culture of governance.

Finally, students have been participants in governance for more than a generation, and they, too, are overlooked; indeed, when one discusses students, the focus is on undergraduates. Graduate students, however, have become increasingly vocal participants in governance, particularly at the departmental and school levels. As graduate student unions continue to increase on private and public campuses, a fruitful line of research will be to see how unionization changes the role of students in their representation, power, and authority in governance.

Communication Matters

Although one might conduct research through any number of disciplinary lenses, if one works from a cultural perspective in a manner akin to what I have sketched here, a particularly germane line of work pertains to the discursive codes through which governance gets enacted. Most research has used the case study method and discussed how organizational structures pertaining to governance function.

An alternative manner of investigation is to look not at structures, but at communication. How do constituencies communicate with one another? Who communicates with whom? In an age when texts and discussion are increasingly mediated by electronic technologies, how does the Internet influence governance? If communication is important for the effectiveness of governance, then is campus governance enhanced by listservs and virtual meetings? Until now, far too much of the research on governance has derived from a structural standpoint. The field also will benefit by standing the typical line of research on its head: rather than tracing the history and changes of structures, study how different groups have communicated about specific issues.

Effectiveness Matters

Whether one bemoans or celebrates calls for shared governance, the assumption is that governance matters. Indeed, in yet another armchair declaration about governance, a celebrated group of academic leaders concluded, "The governance of universities is becoming increasingly crucial" (Hirsch & Weber, 2001, p. vii), not just within the United States but throughout the world. In an earlier section, I argued that one needs to have indicators of effectiveness for governance. At the outset of the text I touched on various interpretations a few analysts had provided about the purpose of governance.

Rosovsky, for example, said that the purpose of governance is to enhance teaching and research, and Trow suggested that one purpose is to remove public institutions from political interference. Regardless of the purposes, no one knows whether, once a purpose has been defined at a college or university, the venues of governance enhance, impede, or are irrelevant to the institution achieving its goal. One could, for example, develop a baseline of indicators for judging quality, select a group of similar institutions, and determine over a five-year time horizon which institutions have gotten better and which have not. A retrospective case study of each institution might lend insight into the role governance plays in institutional improvement.

To be sure, there are any number of methodological stumbling blocks with such a scenario. However, at present, the field is virtually devoid of any form of comparative or longitudinal analysis. Indeed, when comparative studies are considered, they focus on U.S. institutions. At a time when globalization has increased the need for greater understanding about how different systems function, there is a particular urgency for comparative research.

In sum, my purpose has been neither to restrict nor encapsulate worthwhile avenues for research. Higher education is currently experiencing as great a time of change as any in the last century. During periods of change, one might not be surprised that studies of leadership occur, or that armchair observers proffer one or another opinion. What is critically needed, however, is to move beyond retrospective observations of the organization or studies of the individual leader, and to consider instead the manner in which postsecondary organizations undertake governance to meet the multiple needs of the 21st century.

References

Alfred, R. L. (1985). Organizing for renewal through participative governance. *New Directions for Higher Education, 13*(1), 57–63.

Amacher, R., & Meiners, R. (2002). *Free the universities: Reforming higher education to keep pace with the information age.* San Francisco: Pacific Research Institute for Public Policy.

American Association for Higher Education (AAHE). (1967). *Faculty participation in academic governance.* Washington, DC: AAHE-NEA Task Force on Faculty Representation and Academic Negotiations.

American Association of University Professors (AAHE). (1971, April). *At the brink: Preliminary report on the economic status of the profession, 1970–71.* Paper presented at the annual meeting of the American Association of University Professors, Philadelphia, PA.

American Association of University Professors (AAUP). (2001). Statement on government of colleges and universities. In *AAUP Policy Documents and Reports* (9th ed.). Washington, DC: Author.

Armstrong, L. (2000). An academic leader's perspective on a disruptive product. *Change, 32*(6), 20–27.

Association of Governing Boards of Universities and Colleges (AGB). (1996). *Renewing the academic presidency: Stronger leadership for tougher times.* Report of the Commission on the Academic Presidency. Washington, DC: Author.

Association of Governing Boards of Universities and Colleges (AGB). (1998, November 8). AGB statement on institutional governance. Retrieved October 13, 1999, from http://www.agb.org/wmspage.cfm?parm1=143

Baldridge, J. V. (Ed.). (1971). Introduction: Models of university governance—bureaucratic, collegial, and political. In *Academic governance: Research on institutional politics and decision making.* Berkeley, CA: McCutchan.

Baldridge, J. V. (1982). Shared governance: A fable about the lost magic kingdom. *Academe, 68*, 12–15.

Beach, J. A. (1985). The management and governance of academic institutions. *The Journal of College and University Law, 12*, 301–341.

Beck, H. P. (1947). *Men who control our universities.* Morningside Heights, NY: King's Crown.

Birnbaum, R. (1988). *How colleges work: The cybernetics of academic organization and leadership.* San Francisco: Jossey-Bass.

Birnbaum, R. (1989). The cybernetic institution: Toward an integration of governance theories. *Higher Education, 18*, 239–253.

Blackwell, E. A., & Cistone, P. J. (1999). Power and influence in higher education: The case of Florida. *Higher Education Policy, 12*, 111–122.

Bowen, W. G. (1994). *Inside the boardroom: Governance by directors and trustees.* New York: John Wiley.

Burgan, M. (1998). Academic citizenship: A fading vision. *Liberal Education, 84*(4), 16–21.

Bylaws: *James E. Beasley School of Law, Temple University.* (n.d.). (Available from the James E. Beasley School of Law, Temple University, 1719 N. Broad Street Philadelphia, PA 19122.)

Chait, R. P. (2002). *The questions of tenure.* Cambridge, MA: Harvard University Press.

Chait, R. P., Holland, T. P., & Taylor, B. E. (1991). *The effective board of trustees.* New York: Maxwell Macmillan International.

Chait, R. P., Holland, T. P., & Taylor, B. E. (1996). *Improving the performance of governing boards.* Phoenix, AZ: ACE/Oryx Press.

Chait, R. P., & Taylor, B. (1989, January–February). Charting the territory of non-profit boards. *Harvard Business Review,* pp. 44–54.

Christensen, C. M. (1997). *The innovator's dilemma: When new technologies cause great firms to fail.* Boston: Harvard Business School Press.

Clark, B. R. (1998). *Creating entrepreneurial universities: Organizational pathways of transformation.* Oxford, UK: Pergamon.

Collis, D. (2000). "When industries change" revisited: New scenarios for higher education. In M. Devlin & J. Meyerson (Eds.), *Forum futures: Exploring the future of higher education* (pp. 103–125). San Francisco: Jossey-Bass.

Corson, J. (1960). *Governance of colleges and universities.* New York: McGraw-Hill.

Dill, D. D., & Helm, K. P. (1988). Faculty participation in strategic policy making. In J. Smart (Ed.), *Higher education: Handbook of theory and research* (Vol. 4, pp. 319–354). New York: Agathon.

Drummond, M. E., & Reitsch, A. (1995, Summer/Fall). The relationship between shared governance models and faculty and administrator attitudes. *Journal for Higher Education Management, 11*(1), 49–58.

Duderstadt, J. J. (2000a). *Fire, ready, aim: University decision making during an era of rapid change.* Paper presented at the Glion Colloquium II, La Jolla, CA.

Duderstadt, J. J. (2000b). *A university for the 21st century.* Ann Arbor, MI: University of Michigan Press.

Duryea, E. D., & Williams, D. (Eds.) (2000). *The academic corporation: A history of college and university governing boards.* New York: Falmer.

Dykes, A. R. (1968). *Faculty participation in academic decision making.* American Council on Education Monograph. Washington, DC: American Council on Education.

Eckel, P. D. (2000). The role of shared governance in institutional hard decisions: Enabler or antagonist? *Review of Higher Education, 24*(1), 15–39.

Ewell, P. T. (Ed.) (1985). *Assessing educational outcomes.* San Francisco: Jossey-Bass.

Ewell, P. T. (1990). *State policy on assessment: The linkage to learning.* Denver, CO: Education Commission of the States.

Frank, R. H. (2000). Higher education: The ultimate winner-take-all market. In M. Devlin & J. Meyerson (Eds.), *Forum futures: Exploring the future of higher education* (pp. 3–12). San Francisco: Jossey-Bass.

Frank, R. H., & Cook, P. J. (1996). *The winner-take-all society: Why the few at the top get so much more than the rest of us.* New York: Penguin.

Gilmour, J. E. (1991a). Participative governance bodies in higher education: Report of a national study. *New Directions for Higher Education, 19*(3), 27–39.

Gilmour, J. E. (1991b). Your faculty senate: More effective than you think? *Academe*, *77*(5), 16–18.

Grant, G., & Riesman, D. (1978). *The perpetual dream: Reform and experiment in the American college.* Chicago: University of Chicago.

Griffith, R. (1993). Budget cuts and shared governance. *Academe*, *79*(6), 15–17.

Hamilton, N. (1997). Peer review: The linchpin of academic freedom and tenure. *Academe*, *83*(3), 5–19.

Hamilton, N. (1999). Are we speaking the same language? Comparing AAUP & AGB. *Liberal Education*, *85*(4), 24–31.

Hardy, C. (1990). Putting power into university academic governance. In J. Smart (Ed.), *Higher education: Handbook of theory and research* (Vol. 4, pp. 393–426). New York: Agathon.

Hardy, C., Langley, A., Mintzberg, H., & Rose, J. (1983). Strategy formation in the university setting. *Review of Higher Education*, *6*, 407–433.

Hirsch, W. Z., & Weber, L. E. (2001). *Governance in higher education: The university in a state of flux.* London: Economica.

Hollinger, D. A. (2001). Faculty governance, the University of California, and the future of academe. *Academe*, *87*(3), 30–33.

Kaplan, G. (2002). *2001 survey on higher education governance.* (Available from the Hauser Center of Nonprofit Organizations, Harvard University, 79 JFK Street, BT 220B, Cambridge, MA 01238.)

Keller, G. (1987). Shotgun marriage: The growing connection between academic management and faculty governance. In J. Schuster & L. Miller (Eds.), *Governing tomorrow's campuses* (pp. 133–140). New York: ACE/Macmillan.

Kezar, A., & Eckel, P. (2002, March). *Meeting today's governance challenges: A synthesis of the literature and examination of a future research agenda.* Paper presented at a meeting of the American Education Research Association conference in New Orleans, LA.

Leatherman, C. (1998, January 30). "Shared governance" under siege: Is it time to revive it or get rid of it? *The Chronicle of Higher Education*, p. A8.

Lee, B. (1991). Campus leaders and campus senates. *New Directions for Higher Education*, *19*(3), 41–61.

Leslie, D. W., & Fretwell, E. K. (1996). *Wise moves in hard times: Creating and managing resilient colleges and universities.* San Francisco: Jossey-Bass.

Letts, C. W., Ryan, W. P., & Grossman, A. (1999). *High performance nonprofit organizations: Managing upstream for greater impact.* New York: John Wiley.

Lewis, L. S. (2000). *When power corrupts: Academic governing boards in the shadow of the Adelphi case.* New Brunswick, NJ: Transaction.

Light, P. (1998). *Sustaining innovation: Creating nonprofit and government organizations that innovate naturally.* San Francisco: Jossey-Bass.

Longin, T. C. (2002). Institutional governance: A call for collaborative decision making in American higher education. In W. G. Berberet & L. A. McMillin (Eds.), *A new academic compact* (pp. 211–221). Bolton, MA: Anker.

Madsen, H. (1997). *Composition of governing boards of independent colleges and universities.* AGB Occasional Paper No. 36. Washington, DC: Association of Governing Boards of Universities and Colleges.

McGrath, E. J. (1936). The control of education in America. *The Educational Record, 17,* 259–272.

McGuinness, A. C. (1994). *State postsecondary education structures handbook.* Denver, CO: Education Commission of the States.

Metzger, W. P. (1987). Academic governance: An evolutionary perspective. In J. Schuster & L. Miller (Eds.), *Governing tomorrow's campuses* (pp. 3–24). New York: ACE/Macmillan.

Miller, M., McCormack, T., & Newman, R. (1996). Faculty involvement in governance: A comparison of two faculties. *The Journal of Staff, Program, and Organization Development, 27,* 180–190.

Millett, J. D. (1962). *Academic community.* New York: McGraw-Hill.

Millett, J. D. (1978). *New structure of campus power: Successes and failures of emerging forms of institutional governance.* San Francisco: Jossey-Bass.

Mortimer, K. P., & McConnell, T. R. (1978). *Sharing authority effectively.* San Francisco: Jossey-Bass.

Nelson, C. (1999, April 16). The war against the faculty. *The Chronicle of Higher Education,* pp. B4–B9.

Pfnister, A. O. (1970). The role of faculty in university governance. *Journal of Higher Education, 41,* 430–449.

Ramo, K. J. (1997). Reforming shared governance: Do the arguments hold up? *Academe, 83*(5), 38–43.

Ramo, K. J. (1998). *Assessing the faculty's role in shared governance: Implications of AAUP standards.* Washington, DC: American Association of University Professors.

Richardson, J. T. (1999, February 12). Centralizing governance isn't simply wrong: It's bad business, too. *The Chronicle of Higher Education,* p. B9.

Richardson, R. C., Jr., Bracco, K. R., Callan, P. M., & Finney, J. E. (1999). *Designing state higher education systems for a new century.* Phoenix, AZ: American Council on Education/Oryx.

Rosovsky, H. (1990). *The university: An owner's manual.* New York: W .W. Norton.

Rosovsky, H. (2001). Some thoughts about university governance. In W. Hirsch & L. Weber (Eds.), *Governance in higher education: The university in flux* (pp. 94–104). London: Economica.

Schuster, J. H., Smith, D. G., Corak, K. A., & Yamada, M. M. (1994). *Strategic governance: How to make big decisions better.* Phoenix, AZ: American Council on Education/Oryx.

Scott, J. V. (1996). The strange death of faculty governance. *PS: Political Science and Politics, 29,* 724–726.

Scott, J. V. (1997). Death by inattention: The strange fate of faculty governance. *Academe, 83,* 28–33.

Sinclair, U. (1923). *The goose-step: A study of American education.* Pasadena, CA: Author.

Taylor, B., Chait, R. P., & Holland, T. (1996, September–October). The new work of the nonprofit board. *Harvard Business Review,* pp. 36–46.

Thomas, S. L., Pusser, B., & Slaughter, S. (2002). *Playing the board game: An empirical analysis of university trustee and corporate board interlocks.* Unpublished manuscript, University of Arizona Center for the Study of Higher Education, Tucson, AZ.

Tierney, W. G. (1983). Governance by conversation: An essay on the structure, function, and communicative codes of a faculty senate. *Human Organization, 42,* 172–177.

Tierney, W .G. (1988). Organizational culture in higher education: Defining the essentials. *Journal of Higher Education, 59*(1), 2–21.

Tierney, W .G. (1991). Academic work and institutional culture: Constructing knowledge. *Review of Higher Education, 14*(2), 201–219.

Tierney, W. G. (1993). *Building communities of difference: Higher education in the 21st century.* Westport, CT: Bergin & Garvey.

Tierney, W .G. (Ed.). (1998). *The responsive university: Restructuring for high performance.* Baltimore, MD: Johns Hopkins University Press.

Tierney, W. G. (1999). *Building the responsive campus: Creating high performance colleges and universities.* Thousand Oaks, CA: Sage.

Tierney, W. G., & Minor, J. (2002). *Challenges for governance.* (Available from the Center for Higher Education Policy Analysis, Rossier School of Education, University of Southern California, WPH 701, Los Angeles, CA 90089-4037.)

Trow, M. (1990). The academic senate as a school for university leadership. *Liberal Education, 76*(1), 23–27.

Trow, M. (1998). Governance in the University of California: The transformation of politics into administration. *Higher Education Policy, 11,* 201–215.

Veblen, T. (1957). *The higher learning in America.* New York: Hill and Wang (original work published 1918).

Williams, D., Gore, W., Broches, C., & Lostoski, C. (1987). One faculty's perceptions of its governance role. *Journal of Higher Education, 58*(6), 629–655.

Wolvin, A. D. (1991). When governance is really shared: The multi-constituency senate. *Academe, 77*(5), 26–28.

INDEX